THE AFRICAN-BUSH PILOT

II

THE AFRICAN-BUSH PILOT

BY
CECIL "MOON" MULLINS

III

The African-Bush Pilot–
Flying Jets in the Jungles of Africa
Copyright © 2012 by Cecil "Moon" Mullins. All rights reserved.

Published by Cecil "Moon" Mullins
www.theafricanbushpilot.com | B727BushPilot@aol.com

Edited by David Wade and Al Morris

Poems by Pat Mullins

Photo imagining by Michael Conatser

Book cover design and text layout/formatting by Eli Blyden
www.CrunchTimeGraphics.net | crunchtimeg@msn.com

ISBN: 978-0-578-10691-5

Biography/Autobiography/Memoir/Aviation/Travel/Africa

Printed in the United States of America:
A&A Printing | www.printshopcentral.com

DEDICATION

My book must be dedicated to my wife and family, who waited patiently for me to come home during all the many years of my traveling around the world, suffering through the hardships of an all-too-frequent absentee husband and father.

I would also like to dedicate my work to my fellow aviation friends who lost their lives flying in the African war zones while we were all there making a living to feed our families: Jack Anderson, who was killed in Angola while flying as flight engineer on a C-130 Hercules cargo carrier; Charles Jacox, John Wilson Jr., Robert Maynard, Charles Kelly from California, and Alex Nicoll of Southampton, England, who lost their lives flying C-97 cargo aircraft in Biafra. Some of these people will also be mentioned in a number of the incidents narrated throughout the book.

These lost-but-not-forgotten friends came from many different locations around the world. Despite language barriers and cultural differences, we all worked together to complete the mission. One of my colleagues, Jack Anderson, also served as flight engineer assigned to the same reserve unit that I was in at Charleston AFB, South Carolina. He personally helped me figure out how to fly a DC-8 with the #2 engine missing and to land successfully in Luanda, Angola's capital city. It took a little time and a "big" bottle of Jack Daniels while sitting under the mango tree and avoiding the shenanigans of a parrot named Henry at our compound to solve this problem, a considerably astounding endeavor—not the consumption of Jack Daniels, mind you, but rather the flying of an aircraft with one missing engine! I'll enlighten you on this incident in a later chapter.

Captain Cecil "Moon" Mullins

CONTENTS

ACKNOWLEDGEMENTS

I decided to write this book for a number of reasons. First of all, as I think anyone would have to agree, this vagabond lifestyle that takes one away from one's family certainly is a hardship and makes it very difficult to maintain a functional family relationship. Second, in order to feed our families, we sometimes have to do things that we may not necessarily want to do. Although I greatly enjoyed a challenging career in aviation, I did miss growing together with my wife and my daughters, and this absence has left a permanent puncture in my heart.

As children grow older, they have even more of a need, I'm now convinced, for close family relationships. And it is woefully inevitable that the missing father creates additional strife. During my vagabond lifestyle, I had a wife, Betty, and two young daughters, Karen and Tammy at home, discovering, to my dismay, that I had another daughter, Teresa, whom I had never seen until a few years ago! I am very fond of her, of course, and wish I could have had her in my heart and soul from the very beginning. Regrettably, as a result of an absentee grandpa that I was, most of the children never really had the opportunity to know and accept me. Sometimes we just have to play the hand that is dealt to us. The book will at least be something my grandkids can cling to—perhaps even displayed proudly in their book shelves—in the future to enlighten them about the life of their opportunity-seeking, risk-taking grandfather.

I was married twice before. Since my first wife and I never really had the chance to figure each other out, I have to agree with the saying, "The first one doesn't really count." The second one divorced me because she could not tolerate my adventurous life as a vagabond. When I began to believe that I had received a KO in the marriage department, my "God Send" showed up, a woman with whom I continue to share true love and devotion.

Speaking of family, my book would not be complete if I failed to note the people who brought me into the world: my father and mother,

Henry R. Mullins and Vesta Mullins. I am sure they often wondered in which direction I would eventually turn my life because a great deal of unpredictably described my misspent youth at home.

Next, I must mention my older sister, Buena Large, whom I loved very dearly. I think she hung on to the notion that I was really *her* little baby when I was born. She never stopped worrying about me and my adventurous life style (bless her heart), and continued her support for me. She went on to a better world about four years ago.

John Caywood, my former high school physics teacher, often nudged me properly forward, serving as my mentor and role model. Through his own aeronautical experience and teachings, I managed to grab hold of the concept of success and accomplishment.

I want to thank two inspiring people with whom I served in the United States Air Force. First of all, Master Sergeant Browning functioned instrumentally in assisting me to acquire my A and P (Airframe & Power Plant) rating in order to become a professional aircraft mechanic. Sgt. Browning further helped me secure a civil service job with the DC Air National Guard. Next, Lt. Col. Moe Foster hired me for a position with the Tennessee ANG. These two individuals led me in the right direction. I only needed to put my best foot forward.

I would also like to thank the Tennessee ANG for its support in allowing me to enter its flying program as a boom operator and flight engineer, both of which represented another stepping stone towards flying the Boeing 707.

Additional thanks go to some of the very best pilots in the world, aviators who perhaps unknowingly spurred me on as I sat close to them watching their every move in my capacity as flight engineer: Mel Cauthen, Robert Akin, Moe Foster, Bob Worrell, Bob Arr, Dale Dyslin, Fred Womack, and Bob Harr, to name a few, ranging from captain to colonel in military ranks at that time, and a number of them retired as generals. Some of these fellows even let me have a little "stick time" occasionally. Had they been caught, they would most certainly have found themselves in "deep doo-doo." I'll highlight some of their roles in my aviation career in other parts of the book.

Mel Cauthen got me the first flying job that put me into the piloting business with Independent Construction Company out of

Chattanooga, Tennessee. I not only worked as pilot for the firm but also as project manager for the construction of shopping centers throughout the South Eastern United States. The company owned a Cessna 210 and two Bonanza aircraft.

Bill Brantley, moreover, recommended me for a position as flight engineer with a cargo airline in Miami, my first shot at flying under a FAR Part 121 (airline regulations) operation. In addition, Roy Harrison supported me tremendously during my initial flight-engineer program.

Of course, I cannot understate the start-to-finish support and the proof reading provided by my wife, Pat, and daughter, Teresa. They both gave me the necessary prod not only to begin the writing project but also to bring it to a conclusion.

I also want to thank those who supported me with the book by providing me with such things as photos, scripts, and general support: George Buero, Mike Buero, Chester Harper, Steve Rodriguez, Bill Stotts, Ray Boutwell, and Julius Aquino. An added acknowledgement goes to Michael Conatser for his artistic photo-imaging work.

Let us not forget the editing prowess of Al Morris (aka Ace Abbot), the author of his own book entitled *The Rogue Aviator: in the back alleys of aviation*, and David Wade, both of whom pushed me to my limits to do this book right. David also put his "photo-shopping touch" to the photos that make up the book's interior.

Then, too, I must thank God for providing me all that was needed to complete this incredible life's adventure that has led to my very first publication.

I choose not elaborate on the very personal things out of my life though I readily admit to living life to the maximum throughout my aviator's days. Because I knew that my life could have ceased any day during dangerous flight conditions, I nonetheless held to such a philosophic approach. I did earn a lot of money those days. I did enjoy to the fullest the little time I spent at home with my family in attempts to make up for lost time. Nowadays, my wife and I we still live very comfortably on the residual and the retirement incomes generated from years of aviation experience.

I truly think that the gentleman up there in the sky has a plan that has allowed me to survive numerous incidents and accidents for a reason. With the exception of family deaths, funerals, and an occasional church attendance with school friends, I did not grace the doors of any house of worship. I figure the big guy "upstairs" has kept me around to permit me the time to spend the remaining years of my life *closer* to the family that I now have.

In conclusion, life has a way of putting you and other people on the same path. When I became involved with members of the American Legion Post 258 in Jonesboro, Georgia, for example, we worked together to start our own little chapel. I thank my family for sticking with me and God for giving me countless chances. As you continue with me on this adventure of my life, I'm sure you will come to understand the full power of this testimony.

INTRODUCTION

This is a book that not only takes you on adventurous flying trips, the narrative also provides more than a glimpse into a world of flying that most pilots today, I'm certain, know nothing about. From the standpoint of those who purchase airline tickets, airline passengers—aside from those unfortunate passengers and other victims connected to 9/11, to terrorist plots, and to other events that bring down airplanes and their innocent victims—are familiar for the most part with the ease of flying, with the enjoyment of catered (and nowadays mostly uncatered) meals, with lots of different flight attendants, with in-flight movies.

This book intends to enlighten you on the non-scheduled, dark-night cargo carriers over the back woods and above Africa's bush. *Air America*, a 1990 film starring Mel Gibson and Robert Downey Jr., offers a screen version of the kind of flying I did in Africa. Unlike the film's characters, however, I never carried out covert air operations for the CIA—at least not to my knowledge.

My story also aims to demonstrate that not all pilots are underworked, overpaid prima donnas, but rather they represent the opposite side of aviation: the freight haulers who go to work at "dark thirty" and don't get to bed until the crack of dawn; the commercial-feeder airline pilots who normally fly at low altitudes where most of the adverse weather is encountered and make very little pay for what they do; and the pilots who fly small aircraft to make up the majority of all flying throughout the world.

Finally, even if you have never before set foot into an aircraft's cockpit, I'm hoping you'll have the ability to *visualize* what it's like to go airborne in an actual war zone: the single most dangerous flying of all.

Fasten your seat belt, hang on tight, and get ready for a wild ride with the African-bush pilot!

CHAPTER ONE
BOYHOOD YEARS

On January 17, 1936, I was born Cecil Mullins, the son of coal miner, in Keith, West Virginia, a very primitive part of the world with very little to do but work in the coal fields. An outsider would have to spend some time in this environment to understand the way people live in this part of the country. Families and relatives, generation after generation, lived lives considerably different than most families nowadays. They were all much more closely unified back then, spending Christmas and most other holidays together, especially Memorial Day, when we all gathered at the family gravesites to pay our respects to those who have gone to the better land before us.

Some of the locals were musicians, including my mother, who played the banjo quite well. We called these assemblies "All day singing and dinner on the ground." My mother was also affiliated with a country music band, which would play at square dances, pie suppers, and other social gatherings. Sometimes a handful of other family members, who were also pickers, would gather at our house on the front porch, where the swing would move to and fro and the rocking chairs would sway back and forth as they played their country songs. Even today I can still hear my mother plucking the old bluegrass song, "Going up Cripple Creek," on her banjo. The first stanza goes like this: "I got a girl and she loves me/She's as sweet as sweet can be/She's got eyes of baby blue/Makes my gun shoot straight and true."

My father started working in the mines when he was only twelve years of age. He and his fellow miners went into the mine before dawn and did not return until after dark. The workers never saw daylight until the weekend. According to him, the standard pay was about fifty cents a day at that time. When World War II broke out, my father volunteered for the Navy, and off he went to fight for our country as did many other men and women in the area. Since these were very trying times, everyone had to make sacrifices. Everyone pitched in to help in one way or the other. My mother had to go to work in order to help support the family. To find a job she had to relocate herself, leaving us kids with our grandmother, part of the price of keeping this country free. America lost close to 500,000 men during that war, including members of my own family, and some ended up crippled for life as a result of wartime injuries.

My father, not spared by war's ravaging hands, returned home before the war ended with a ninety-percent disability. Military doctors advised him that he would never be able to work again. Not willing to yield to his disability, my father did not take them seriously and purchased a military surplus dump truck, and so began his coal-hauling business.

Day after day I watched him go to work with his twisted back to us. Physically, it didn't appear that he would be able to work at anything—but he continued on. He was a hell of a man! There was not a word in his vocabulary that had anything to do with quitting. Then, too, for many of the tough, old mountain men, a bottle of liquor followed by a good old-fashioned street brawl was a common occurrence. I followed my father around like a little puppy dog.

My Dad hauled coal all day long. During the evenings after work, he spent lots of time repairing his old clunker of a truck. Naturally, I was right there handing him tools and watching his every move. As a result of that experience, I discovered my own mechanical inclination. Of course, I had lots of mechanical work to do for myself on a couple of bicycles that I maintained. I needed two bicycles since I frequently had to cannibalize parts from one bike to keep a good bike on the road.

My father finally graduated into the coal-mining business. Along with one of his uncles who helped in the financing, they purchased what they called "a piece of coal." Then he started bringing in the big bucks. He purchased our first house, and with hard work and frugality, the house was paid off in five years. As I remember, my father was a man who did not like to owe anything to anybody. I more or less shadowed both my father and my uncle until I got into high school, which then took up most of my time.

I wasn't the best student by any means. I even quit school one year. My father then gave me an ultimatum: if I had no intention to continue high school, then I would have to go to work in the coal mines—which

I did. He gave me a number five coal shovel, which is the largest size used. I think he planned all along to get me to change my mind and to coerce me to go back to school. However, I continued the manual labor for a while.

I was the *richest* kid in the pack because I could load nearly twenty-one coal cars a day at one dollar per car. This resulted in about $100 a week in income, which was really big money during that period, earning about as much money per week as those men who did the same job and raised a family at the same time!

Aside from the joy at taking home such a lavish amount of money each week, I can still remember the cracking noises of the mines, caused by the shifting of the ground. Such unholy creaks, moans, and groans would have to make the average person leery about climbing down into those deep, dark holes. Other than subsistence farming and hunting, there was unfortunately no other reasonable source of income.

I remember the times when the mine inspector came around. My Dad would send someone to tell me to scoot immediately to the drift mouth (where the big fan that circulates the air throughout the mine is located). I would then exit the mine and jog to the top of the hill out of sight of the inspector. I was only sixteen at the time. The inspector, I figure even now, would most likely have closed down the mine had I been caught working there.

I managed to tolerate the unholy creaks. However, the big slate falls, gas explosions, and other accidents in these dark and dreary holes left a much greater impression in my head. Fueled by carbide, the lanterns— the miners' only lighting system attached to their hardhats—most likely caused many of the gas explosions, together with poor ventilation. Lots of miners lost their lives because of these problems. My father had experienced several slate falls himself, fortunately surviving all of them. Some of my uncles, on the other hand, were not so lucky.

On top of all the bad things that made up the miners' lives underground, safety standards were very lax in those days. In fact, many miners lost their lives to the dreadful monster called the "black lung." Clearly, I had it in my head *not* to make this an occupation for the rest of my life. In short time, I left the mines to resume my academic studies.

Some of my Dad's Coal-Miner friends

Coal Tipple at Coalwood, West Virginia

Aside from all the nasty aspects of mining life, many of my friends and I liked to indulge in beer and wine. Such an indulgence, of course, led to a lot of things that were not in the best interests of parents—or anyone else for that matter. Alcoholic consumption was just a way of life in that "neck of the woods," as the old cliché goes.

Obviously, we also became interested in the opposite sex. Control devices, other than the old-fashioned condom, were not yet available, and many of us got in trouble, including me. I did not learn of the results of this sowing of wild oats until many years later. Reckless sex and reckless driving inevitably led to a badge of honor, namely to "total" one's car. In my senior year of high school, I had eight auto accidents! Several of them were "totals."

Me, Bobby Taylor, "Bear" Fleming, and "Chicken" Stanley

"The Motley Crew"

Luckily for me, a mentor showed up just in time to keep me from sliding off the slippery slope into the muddy ditches that young men frequently end in when their thoughts, like irresponsible auto accidents, wind up totaled along the side of some road. The man who appeared in my life turned out to be a new physics teacher named John Caywood. Previously employed by the Martin Aircraft Company, Mr. Caywood impressed me considerably with his knowledge of those subjects that related to aviation. For the first time in my life, a brand new light bulb lit up my brain! I discovered an interest that I wanted to pursue. Mr. Caywood's teachings, linked tightly to the sleek, new Boeing 707s gleaming overhead, inspired me to fly that big jet myself one day. The Boeing 707 was the most beautiful airplane I had ever seen, creating a vision that would one day fulfill itself.

CHAPTER TWO
"OFF WE GO INTO THE WILD BLUE YONDER!"

United States Air Force

I finally got it all together and finished high school, knowing that I was definitely not going to work in the coal industry for the rest of my life. In fact, I don't mind comparing myself to the main, teenaged character in the movie *October Sky*. The film is based on a teenager who grows up in a coal town in West Virginia, where a boy's accepted destiny would have him ending "up in the mines." Just as I had my eye oriented to the sky to command the flight of jet aircraft, the film's character had his eye on the sky in his love of creating and flying rockets. Our lives, moreover, were both greatly influenced by high school teachers. I fulfilled my own destiny, and the "rocket boy" went on to become a success story as rocket scientist with the NASA program. My cousin, Kendrick King went to school with the gentleman, whose name is Homer Hickam.

With the conclusion of high school, three buddies and I decided to enlist in the United States Air Force. Wright Carter, Dean Anderson, Stacy Lockhart, and I hopped on the train and lit out for San Antonio, Texas, to begin basic training at Lackland Air Force Base. When we met our official training instructor (TI), we soon found out that our military lifestyle would take a significant leap from our civilian lifestyle back in Virginia.

On a daily basis, it was all "Yes, sir!" or "No, sir!" from the get-go–and no questions in between. I had already spent about a year in the Army Reserves, so I was somewhat familiar with how to play the game. Because of my previous military experience, the TI assigned me to serve as his assistant, which often left me in charge of marching the troops around the parade field with my own personally devised cadence: "We had a good home, but we left, right, left, right." We would normally march around for an hour. At break time, we'd find a field off the road somewhere to take a "Smoke-'em-if-you-got-'em break." We also received instructions on the classic military concept of "Field stripping your cigarettes": a simple act of tearing apart the cigarette so that it would not start a fire or trash the area.

This extra-duty effort didn't pay me any more money, but occasionally I might get an extra beer or two at the beer garden. We often had what was referred to as "GI parties" in the barracks. Unfortunately, these parties consisted of intense cleaning sessions on our hands and knees on the floor, scrubbing until everything became squeaky clean. Although we did not enjoy this activity, we did learn a few pointers about future roles as house husbands.

Everyone learned to march in step and to shine their shoes. At the end of basic training, we sewed on our first stripe as airmen third class and headed off to a variety of technical schools in order to prepare for our career specialty in the Air Force. To my good fortune, I received an assignment to the jet-mechanic school based in Amarillo, Texas, requiring a long Greyhound bus ride through the Texas Panhandle past tumbleweed after tumbleweed to reach this destination located in the middle of nowhere.

Even though Amarillo sat there as the largest city in West Texas, one could not call this a garden spot. Nevertheless, after several weeks of very intense and demanding training, I completed the aircraft-mechanic school. Of course, during the training I continued to set my mind on climbing into the cockpit of that big, sleek Boeing 707.

I'm certain that Mr. Caywood, my previous physics teacher from high school, would have been proud of me, considering that I finished at the top of my class. As a result of this accomplishment, I had two possible choices: I could attempt to become an aviation cadet in pilot school, or I could pick my first actual base assignment. I thought this over for a couple of days and then probably made the biggest mistake of my life. I really wanted the aviation career; however, I made the mistake that lots of young men do, allowing myself to let the intoxication of romance overrule good judgment. I had this beautiful, petite girlfriend back home, so I went for the base closest to home to be near her. As fate would have it, I finally lost her and have spent an entire lifetime regretting that decision, a bad one at that time. Once the situation sorted itself out, I finally did slip into the captain's chair of that big, sleek Boeing 707.

I think a friend named Wright Carter probably benefited most from his Air Force training. He dotted his "eyes" and crossed his "tees," ending up in the Pentagon with a very high government-service (GS) rating as a civil-service employee. As a matter of fact, Carter helped develop the instrument landing system (ILS) system that is used today at airports all over the world for landing in low visibility and ceiling. The reliability and the accuracy of the ILS system is the only reason that jets can be landed at Heathrow airport during those very frequent periods of pea-soup fog engulfing the airport.

CHAPTER THREE
"NOTED OUTSTANDING UNIT"

The Tennessee Air National Guard (TANG)

As I noted earlier, I first entered into military service as an Army reservist while still in high school in Clintwood, Virginia, in 1955. I then joined the U.S. Air Force in 1956 and continued my military connection until a final retirement in 1996 at the age of sixty with the U.S. Air Force Reserves at the rank of a Master Sergeant (E-7). The United States Air Force was very good to me, even providing me with a little bit of retirement pay—whether I deserved it or not. I also have the right to use VA medical facilities for my health needs, which nowadays I use quite often at my young age of seventy-six.

Interestingly enough, I was offered a commission at one time, the rank of major actually, because of my age at the time. I suppose no one wanted to see a middle-aged 2nd lieutenant wandering around the base. I remained a major, however, for about one month until someone determined that I could not fill the position due to the fact that I did not have the required college credits. Perhaps it was just as well since I *still* had my mind set on a flying position.

During the last year of my initial four-year hitch with the US Air Force, I found myself stationed at Andrews Air Force Base near Washington, DC. To obtain a license that would allow me to perform maintenance on civilian aircraft, I attended a civilian Airframe and Power Plant school (A&P). I later went on to acquire all of the flight-engineer ratings. These ratings—reciprocating, turbo prop, and jet—were needed in order to become a flight-crew member on the flight deck of larger aircraft. Even though he sits in the cockpit, the flight engineer is often not pilot rated and does not have access to the flight controls. He is, however, a critical element on the flight deck since he is in control of most of the aircraft systems during emergency situations, often the decisive player.

On my weekends off, I would jump into my little 1956 Chevy Bel Air Sport Coupe and head for the coal-field mountains of Southwest Virginia to spend time with my new wife, whom I would not normally see, but there were always lots of other darlings for a stopover here and there. My pride and joy at the time, the Chevy sported a two-tone green paint job and a souped-up engine boasting two four-barrel carbs. As a result of the vacuum in both carbs, you could actually see the hood drop a little when I put the pedal to the metal. My parents had given me a '53 four-door Chevy when I finished high school, but the car didn't last very long once I laid my eyes on this beauty, all taking place at the start of the muscle-car days when the gas at the pump also ran less than twenty-five cents per gallon.

Following my discharge from the Air Force, I also acquired an Airline Transport Rating (ATP) with four type-ratings: L-188 (Electra), B-727, B-707/720, and DC-8. These type ratings allowed me to function as a captain on those aircraft. During the remainder of my career, I had the opportunity to fly them all in many different situations around the world, but most notably in my African-bush-pilot adventures.

My actual position at Andrews Air Force Base called for me to work transit alert, an assignment that allowed me front-view action at a place where transient aircraft would pass. While in this position, I got to know many of the people at the DC Air National Guard unit based at Andrews. They talked me into trying for a civil-service position with their unit once I had completed my four years with the Air Force.

During my service time at Andrews, I started pilot training with some cousins who lived in Alexandria, Virginia. They owned a small Aeronica Champ, which they flew out of Hyde Field in Maryland. We would spend most of our weekends there.

I had served for the DC Air National Guard for nearly a year when the maintenance commander from the Tennessee Air National Guard came for a meeting at the Pentagon. When the aircraft commander got ready to leave, he experienced difficulty firing up the F-104's engine. Naturally, I asked if I could help. I pointed out that the wind up the tailpipe was too strong and that I would go to transit alert to fetch a tow bar to turn the aircraft around *into* the wind, confident that this technique would work, and it worked fine. Once the engine had successfully fired up, the commander motioned for me to come up the ladder to talk to him. He then asked me if I would like to have a job with his unit in Tennessee. I accepted this gracious offer, and off I went to Tennessee, the homeland of Davy Crockett.

I had served with the Tennessee Guard unit for only a very short period when we were suddenly recalled to active duty for the Berlin Crisis in 1961. To make a long, complicated story shorter, the Berlin Crisis, according to one internet web site, "involved a controversy so bitter and so sustained that at its height world leaders feared that a misstep could trigger a nuclear war."

In a speech delivered on July 25, 1961, President John F. Kennedy argued, "In Berlin, as you recall, he [Premier Nikita Khrushchev] intends to bring to an end, through a stroke of the pen, first our legal rights to be in West Berlin and secondly our ability to make good on our commitment to the two million free people of that city. That we cannot permit." Kennedy also noted, "Let me remind you that the fortunes of war and diplomacy left the free people of West Berlin, in 1945, 110 miles behind the Iron Curtain."

And what person who lived through this crisis cannot recall what Kennedy personally said on June 26, 1963, to West Berlin citizens gathered to see this American president and to hear his words? With some 450,000 West Berliners present, Kennedy declared, "*Ich bin ein Berliner*," which actually translates idiomatically to "I'm a jelly donut." Despite the unintended humor and the isolating Wall that had been erected almost two years earlier completely around West Berlin, Kennedy, pragmatic about the Wall, said, "It's not a very nice solution, but a wall is a hell of a lot better than a war."

In the meantime, those of us with the Tennessee Guard had to disassemble each of our F-104 aircraft so they would fit into C-124s or C-133s for transport to the Ramstein Air Force Base in what was then West Germany. The whole process of disassembly required thirty days of preparation before the first flight launched for West Germany, where we were stationed for almost a year. Open to a boast here and there, I'm pleased to say that our unit broke several flying records that are still held to this very day. I still acknowledge pride in having been a part of the whole affair.

"Open a little wider, Big Boy!"

In Ramstein, Germany, and ready to fly

After we returned from West Germany, we took delivery of KC-97 refueling tankers. These aircraft were equipped with four 4360 reciprocating engines and two J-47-25 jet engines. I maintained a position as an aircraft mechanic while also flying as the refueling boom operator and flight engineer. Our primary mission consisted of supporting the U.S. Air Force for in-flight refueling over Europe. We would stay at the Rhein-Main Air Base near Frankfurt, West Germany, a U.S. air base that concluded its American commitment in 2005.

It was very unusual to fly this KC-97 aircraft without having some kind of mechanical problem. Each of the four engines had twenty-eight cylinders and fifty-six spark plugs. It was not uncommon to return from a flight with at least one engine shutdown. It was also an aircraft that required the flight engineer to have a very good mechanical knowledge of the aircraft systems.

By way of example, we experienced a problem with the aircraft-pressurization system during an Operational Readiness Inspection (ORI). I served as the flight engineer. For a while it looked as if we were going to have to abort the flight and end up with a bad report card on the ORI. Not a person to turn aside from a challenge, I asked the aircraft commander to keep climbing and to use oxygen if necessary to give me a chance to try to fix the problem.

I checked the aircraft maintenance logbook, discovering that the electricians had been working on a problem with the landing gear. Quite familiar with this system, I knew that the landing gear had an oleo switch that controlled the pressurization systems. The oleo switch determined if we were on the ground or in the air and if the gear was up or down. Luckily, when I tinkered with the oleo switch, the system then went into the air mode, and the aircraft pressurized normally. We continued the mission and passed the ORI with flying colors.

I can recall other occasions when I was able to keep the aircraft going to complete missions as a result of my maintenance experience. One such incident involved a refueling stop at Goose Bay, Labrador. It was an exceptionally cold and snowy day. There were several airplanes waiting for fuel and it took much longer than normal to get us refueled.

We finally got the aircraft fueled after two hours of waiting. We started the reciprocating engines and taxied to the end of the runway for takeoff. The copilot received our air-traffic-control (ATC) clearance, and we were all ready to go. It was standard practice to wait until just before takeoff to start the two jet engines (a fuel consumption consideration). The first engine started normally. The second chose to take a time out. We tried a few more times with no success and then went back to ramp.

The aircraft commander, Major Mel Cauthen, was one of my favorite aircraft commanders (A/Cs). I asked Mel if he would let me try something that I thought might fix the problem. He was also the same guy who stood by me in another incident during an ORI. He leaned over to tell me to "Do your thing."

These particular engines had igniter plugs that were installed very close to each other in the combustion can. I knew that sometimes they would get burned off at the point, and, when it gets really cold, they will not contact enough, because they are not close enough to each other to create a spark for ignition. I decided to take one of the plugs out of the engine that started normally and installed it in the one that was faulty to see if we could get it started. After about one hour of working in the bitter cold weather to accomplish this task, we were ready to try it. Both engines kicked in and we were able to get underway to Europe. Needless to say, after we landed in West Germany, I did not have to buy any beers, and my *Bierstein* remained constantly replenished.

Here we are on another day with another incident. This one happened at the same place as the previous one. Why is it that bad things happen when the weather is "colder than a witch's tit on an iceberg"? Upon start, a fire-warning light suddenly illuminated on the number three engine. Naturally, we shut the engine down right away, and the warning light immediately went out, indicating there was no actual fire. We really had no clue about what had happened, so I had to go check it out. Once again, I had to go out into the freezing-cold weather to find a ladder in order to climb up to the front of the engine to try to spot anything unusual. I discovered that an "H" link had been pulled off of the exhaust stack on the engine, all of which allowed a hot-air spill against the thermocouple, and in turn, setting off the fire alarm. To fix the problem, we would have to have an exhaust stack and a maintenance stand to get up to the engine.

The A/C and I decided that I should go down to the maintenance facility to see if maintenance people could help us. We also needed to call base ops (operations) to report the problem. Good fortune came our way because the facility happened to have war readiness material (WRM) available. The non-commissioned officer in charge (NCOIC) of the facility said that he couldn't remove the parts we needed unless he was authorized by higher authority. Our A/C explained our problem to him and also advised him that we had another flight that was coming through the next day for the same mission and that we could bring a replacement part at that time. The NCOIC then got on the phone with his commander and a part delivery was authorized.

After we received the part, our next obstacle was to replace the faulty one on the aircraft in freezing weather. I could not do the job myself, so one of the avionic technicians who was traveling with us volunteered to help me. His name was Glynn Bounds, and we would eventually become good friends. We could only stand the cold for about a half hour at a time; therefore, we would enter the toasty-warm aircraft every thirty minutes to thaw out. To make a change on this component was difficult, but even more so in adverse weather. We finally did "get 'er done" and continued on our merry way back to West Germany. I found out later from Glynn that one of the reasons he was so ready to help was because he had a little German girlfriend to whom he had given his estimated time of arrival (ETA). The plan called for both of them to meet on the base when he arrived. You might say he had an ulterior motive.

"Fill 'er up and don't forget the Green Stamps"

In-flight refueling, I'm quick to say, could be a very unsafe operation at times. I had several close calls when I flew as boom operator. With a chill running up and down my spine, I remember once catching sight of an F-84 aircraft making its way right under us with the boom still attached! Harold Bishop was manning the boom at the time. We used either drogue or stiff-boom refueling, depending on what type of aircraft we were refueling. The F-84 passed right underneath us while still connected to the boom. The extended section of the boom broke completely off, I observed, as the F-84 passed beneath us, and the broken portion of the boom went to the rear.

Needless to say, our refueling operations for that day came to an immediate halt. When the boom first broke, we still had fuel gushing out of the boom, so Harold immediately ordered the flight engineer to shut the fuel valve off. However, we still had another problem in that the broken boom, now a "torqued dork," could not be stowed in the off position. Therefore, he had to ride in the boom pod to hold the boom up for landing until we came to a dead stop in the parking area. Sometimes you just do what you have to do in order to solve problems that Murphy's Law likes to throw at you.

I recall an incident involving the refueling of an F-100 aircraft. Known as the "lead-sled," the F-100 was somewhat underpowered. During the refueling process, they would become so heavy that they could not maintain speed, and it became necessary to engage in what was referred to as the "toboggan maneuver," namely to initiate a descent with the tanker aircraft in order to increase air speed. The maneuver allowed the F-100 to continue on the boom with the increased speed and therefore to continue the refueling process.

Occasionally, the refueling took place during turbulence and this made it even more difficult. For the receiver aircraft, which are usually fighter jets, refueling at night in the clouds in turbulence was very possibly the most demanding thing a pilot could to. A common response from the pilots after getting their fuel was "Thanks for the fill up and don't forget the green stamps!" One has to be a "baby-boomer," or older, in order to understand "green stamps."

We had yet another extremely cold-weather operation. This occurred when we had to relocate from Tennessee to support an Alabama based fighter unit that was going to be transferred to Anchorage, Alaska. The weather chilled down so much during an overnight park that the cold stiffness of the oil alone did not permit engine start. Compounding our difficulties to get the aircraft running, the refueling tanks were connected together by fuel lines and clamps, resulting in multiple leaks as a result of the cold contracting the lines. The only thing we could do was to try to round up enough heating units for the engines to warm the oil enough to be able to start the engines.

While we were heating the engines, the maintenance people were working hard to stop all of the fuel leaks. We finally got everything thawed out and completed the mission. We did, however, learn our lesson, and from then on we used the fuel-oil-dilution procedure by diluting oil with fuel to assure the engines would start the next morning. If you ever go to cold country, don't forget to thin your oil and drink lots of antifreeze. A frequent phrase expressed by the flight engineer was "Don't push your throttle in too far and stretch her jugs." The term "jugs" was a slang term for the engine's cylinder head. If you increase the manifold pressure too much, the cylinder bolts would actually stretch and cause the cylinder to loosen, which, in turn, would result in a very tangible amount of lost compression and engine power.

KC-97s In Edmonton, Canada—Temperature -40 degrees!

During a warmer-weather excursion to Torrejon Air Force Base, located quite close to Madrid, Spain, we were able to stretch out our imaginations. Our mission had us conducting refueling missions for the Air Force fighter squadrons that were based there. A very good friend of mine named Ray Boutwell, a fellow cockpit crewmember, and I decided we should go to Madrid to explore the area. Rather than using the on-base housing, we went straight to the Hilton Hotel, which sat splendidly right in the center of the city and gave us a perfect location to get around taking in the city's sights.

On the first night there, we headed down to the lounge for some libations. As we sat there enjoying our drinks, this tall guy with denim clothes and cowboy boots entered the lounge. Ray and I looked at each other, and I said, "That guy looks like Robert Mitchum." When he got a little closer, Ray responded, "I'll be go to hell! That *is* Robert Mitchum!"

You would have to know Ray to believe what he said next. He had had a few drinks by now, and the inhibitions were breaking down. Ray turned to the man and said, "Hey Slick." Mitchum responded, "Are you talking to me?" And it appeared that the bar-room brawl would shortly be under way. Ray answered, "Yes!" Mitchum came back with, "Where are you from, boy?" He had tuned into Ray's southern accent. Ray said, "Mississippi." Mitchum gave us a friendly look and said, "I'm from South Carolina," and the southern boys immediately bonded.

Mitchum then asked us what we were doing in Spain. After we informed him that we were supporting U.S. Air Force units based in Torreon, we at once became friends for life. He asked us if we would like to join him in his suite on the third floor. This surely was an invitation not to turn down. Mitchum was there filming the movie *Villa Rides!* Yul Brenner played the chief role of Poncho Villa while Mitchum and Charles Bronson fit in as co-stars, along with a beautiful young actress named Maria Grazia Buccella. The film centered on a revolution with the help of an American aviator. Not wanting to part company with us, Mitchum invited us to accompany him the next day. We agreed, not believing that he really meant it. We finished our drinks and dinner and went to our rooms.

At about five the next morning, the phone rang. I answered, and to my surprise someone yelled out, "Where in the hell are you guys? You were supposed to be here to go to the set with me!" At first, I brushed off the man's scolding, explaining that we had overslept. But then recognizing the voice and realizing the sincerity of Mitchum's invitation, I said we would join him right away.

I shook old Ray awake, and we were off to Mitchum's pad. When we arrived for the breakfast, we could barely believe our eyes. There in front of our shocked eyes sat a large table decked out with everything imaginable to eat and drink. Just a few minutes later, Maria Grazia Buccella entered to join us. Although she entered with another actor, Mitchum invited Maria to our table. He immediately asked, "Did you get laid last night?" Apparently used to his dirty-old-man ways, she passed it off as if he had given her a normal good-morning greeting. Since Mitchum was a serious music fan, he got out his tape of Roger Miller's songs. He said that it was the best music he ever listened to and that Roger Miller had given it to him personally.

We got ready to go and noticed that we did not have our heavy coats with us. It was early in the morning and very cold. We told Mitchum that we didn't think he was serious about us actually going to the set with him and left our coats in our room. He then pulled out a couple of really nice jackets to use. He wanted to get on the road right away and said he did not have the time for a trip to our room to get our own jackets.

Off we went to the movie set. Mitchum still kidded Maria all the way to the desert where they were filming. This was the first time Ray and I had set foot on a movie set located way out in the desert where an old train sat on tracks. An equally old airplane lay there as well, and, of course, the large-format cameras held my flying buddy and me spellbound. The construction crew had also fashioned a barn-like shelter with a roof over it, permitting a shaded place where the crews were able to get out of the sun to enjoy their lunch and coffee breaks. Watching Mitchum make the movie turned out to be an interesting event. However, when I later saw the film, I thought it was just a mediocre piece of work.

CHAPTER FOUR

FLIGHT INSTRUCTING

On the civilian side during the late 1960s or early 1970s, I kept up my flight training at Smokey Mountain Aero, a fixed-base operator on the other side of this dual military and civilian airport known as McGhee Tyson Airport in Knoxville, Tennessee. I became an instructor and flew part time trying to build flying time for my future endeavors. At that time, lots of people took advantage of their GI bill, which paid for their flight training. Aerobatics was a part of that training. I would take all the students for the aerobatic and multi-engine training, as that was what I enjoyed doing the most.

I recall one time when my father was in a mining-slate fall that put him in the hospital at Bluefield, West Virginia. I took one of my multi-engine students on a cross-country flight in a twin-engine Piper Aztec to see my Dad. The weather was no problem on the way up there, but after visiting my Dad for a couple of hours, I returned to the airport intending to depart. A weather check confirmed possible icing between 3000 and 6000 feet. I really needed to get back to Knoxville, so I took a shot at it.

After takeoff, I heard a Piedmont flight report icing at those same altitudes. I still kept going and upon reaching about 3000 feet, the ice accumulated so fast that there was no time to change my mind about doing anything. I reported the problem to the controller, and he asked me if I wanted to return to the airport. By that time I had stopped picking up ice, but the engines were running very roughly due to carburetor icing. I pulled on the carburetor heat and the black smoke literally bellowed out of the exhaust pipes. I pushed back until the black smoke dissipated.

The engines appeared to be holding their own, and the aircraft was flying okay with the added power input. I then advised the controller that I would continue on to Knoxville. I figured if I returned, I would pick up the same amount of ice on the descent as in the climb. Then, too, by going on, I was traveling south, and the temperature would probably get warmer. Lady Luck again smiled upon me because the temperature grew warmer about the time I started the descent into Knoxville. It was just another one of those clean-your-pants situations. Admittedly though, lots of people do get killed flying in those icing conditions around mountainous areas.

In one particular incident, time and motion seemed to stop. At the time, I did some part-time flying for the University of Tennessee, along with some other people who owned airplanes but did not fly: lawyers, contract engineers, and anyone else who needed a pilot. Actually, I had a very good reputation around that area as a part-time pilot. The incident involved a University of Tennessee geology professor who contacted me to fly him to the Smokey Mountains to do some studies.

The wind blew wildly on the day I took him there. I flew him in a Cessna 172 to the desired area situated on the leeward side of the mountains. He got his camera and equipment out and started to do his studies of the area. I think he had something along the line of infra-red imagining. It appeared to me that he was simply taking pictures of the area. We were flying along, sitting there fat, dumb and happy, when he made the statement that this was great, as though we were sitting still, he said. That got my immediate attention. I looked it over and, sure enough, we were sitting still! We were not moving forward, but we were also descending towards the ground. I increased the power and tried to climb the airplane, but we were not going anywhere but down. The wind had become so strong that it was causing us to descend. I knew I had to do something fast, or we would soon find ourselves dangling somewhere in the trees—if we were that lucky.

I made the decision to turn to go with the wind the opposite way to get out of the leeward down draft and then to climb back up far enough to make sure I could get back across the mountains. I finally got far enough away to a point where the airplane would climb. When we reached 10,000 feet, I wanted to be sure I had enough altitude to get back across the area, since I anticipated more down draft on the way. Yes, we made it back intact, but this one definitely turned into another "Clean your pants situation." The lesson learned was to watch the mountain flying, especially at night, when all you can see are the instruments.

In yet another incident, I had taken off from Knoxville one day on an instrument flight. I think I was going across the mountains to Charlotte, North Carolina. Everything was fine for a while, but then all of a sudden I lost my air-speed indications that worked off the pitot tube. I had practiced this in-flight situation with another flight instructor in my training. I used the power and attitude indicator and the sound of the air across the fuselage to determine the airspeed. I think I was flying at an altitude of about 5000 feet when it happened.

Because of my previous experience with this situation, I was able to have the approach controller vector me around to the final-approach course. I employed the distance, along with the attitude indicator, for the three-degree-glide-slope power setting, and used sound for speed control and got the airplane back on the ground. This one didn't even cause a pants-cleaning situation. As it turned out, the problem was a mud dauber (wasp) in the pitot tube. Mr. Wasp, if he could think at all, probably wished he had built his house elsewhere.

We were doing some aerial photography one day for a shopping center company out of Chattanooga, Tennessee. The Tennessee company contracted us to do aerial shots of its grand opening at Murphysboro, Tennessee. My partner, the photographer on this aerial mission, and I flew around the center with the right window open, allowing him to direct me to position the airplane for the best photo shots. The window stayed fully open all the way to the bottom of this high-winged airplane as a result of the wind. Suddenly, we both heard a "Whoooom" noise, followed by a really roughly running engine. I thought we had come into contact with some birds, but that wasn't the case as the engine did not smooth up at all.

The noise actually got worse, the airspeed dropped off, and we held our altitude without stalling the airplane. I knew that the airport was close by, so I looked around and reckoned about a half mile represented the distance between us and the airport. We were about 3,000 feet, and the airport's elevation amounted to about 1,000 feet. As a result, we had some 2,000 feet to play with in trying to make it to the airport. I turned the airplane to head toward the airport and lined us up on a straight-in for the runway.

All we needed now was enough engine power to get us to the airport. We had no other options as the runway was closer than any roads adequate for landing, and the landscape below was dotted with houses everywhere. We, the photographer and I, kept our composure, the airspeed held just above stall speed, and the little airplane gave a sign that we could make it in, that is to say, if nothing else happened. By the skin of our teeth and by the grace of God, we made it. We got on the ground, taxied to the ramp, went to clean our pants, and took a well deserved break. If we had been any farther away from the airport, I seriously doubt we would have made it through this scenario alive. As they say in the aviation world, "Small airplanes are the safest thing in the world; they can only barely kill you."

After the break, we returned to the plane and removed the cowling, noticing an excessive amount of oil on one of the intake valve covers, indicating a possible problem with that particular valve, which we found to be true after removing the cover and discovering that the engine had "swallowed" a valve guide, a term used when the valve separates itself from the holding-spring lock clip. We could do nothing else except to round up the parts, to return, and to fix the problem. We picked up the required parts, returned the next day, fixed the problem, and flew back to McGee Tyson Airport.

I lived to write about another situation—this time on a seafood-hauling fiasco with my partner, Glynn Bounds, in our Cessna 210. Glynn and I headed for Mobile, Alabama, to pick up a load of fresh seafood to sell out of our little seafood store that we operated at the time. We normally flew to Myrtle Beach for this task, but we wanted some good, fresh oysters, and Mobile was the place to get them. We had orders for several bushels and needed to get some for ourselves. We also picked up several extra items we thought we could carry. After loading all of these goods onto the airplane, we noticed that the nose wheel barely touched the ground, indicating that we were tail heavy. There really was not much we could do about it since we had already bought and paid for the load. The Cessna was so tail heavy, you could almost lift the front of the airplane off the ground with one finger! To get rid of some of the load was out of the question, so we proceeded.

Once Glynn and I had boarded, the nose dropped a little, but I knew we were very tail heavy, with no clue about the center of gravity or the lift.

My little "Flying Toy"—the Cessna 210

During the taxi over the humps on the grassy strip, the Cessna's nose would continually lift somewhat off the ground. I took the plane to the very end of the runway and then some "for the wife and kids." With no idea how heavy we were or even if the airplane would fly at all, we added as much power as it would produce and started the takeoff roll. The Cessna lumbered along as though it did not want to get us airborne. I held the pedal to the metal as the end of the runway, including a bunch of intimidating trees, quickly approached!

Finally, the airplane lifted off the ground, and we were able to establish a slight climb. The trees, larger than life itself, *still* stood tall above us at this point, and turning left or right would not have helped. I then raised the landing gear only to realize my mistake because the airplane started to drift down to a *lower* altitude! Now it was "pucker-factor time," and there was absolutely nothing to do but wait and hope we would get over the tree tops. Once the wheels were in the well, the 210 began to climb again, but still not enough to clear the tree tops completely. Now in a helpless position, we hit the tree tops with a big

"Whoooosh!" I thought Glynn was going to *leap* out of his seat! And then it was all over. No, we didn't crash; instead, the airplane very slowly climbed out and away from our close encounter enough to make it back to Knoxville, Tennessee. From then on we checked the approximate weight of the load before trying this stunt again.

Aviators certainly have their stories to tell, and here's an added incident. Al, a friend of mine who owned a restaurant business, had become the owner of a Cessna 210. I don't know if he bought it or won it in a poker game: one way or the other, though, he couldn't fly the thing. He wanted to take a trip to visit some relatives in Columbus, Ohio, asking me if I would like to go with him and do the flying and maybe give him some lessons at the same time. It sounded good to me as he intended to foot all the expenses. I never liked to turn down a free layover trip, especially a flying one.

Al's Cessna 210 was a *really* nice plane, with an almost fresh-off-the-assembly-line look. The airport we were going to land at was the Ohio State University campus airport, a little grass strip with lots of noticeable ruts along the snow cover. The air strip was also located to the rear of Al's family-owned motel, which had both restaurant and lounge. All we had to do was park the airplane and walk to the motel.

We were greeted well on arrival, one of those family-hugging-and-kissing reunions. After all the mushy stuff stopped, we were invited to the bar for a beverage of choice. We had one, then another, another, another until we quit counting. I could see right away that I liked this family, particularly the pretty-lady cousins. Al's folks really knew how to make a guy feel right at home, very easy for me, considering, too, all the available amenities. The surf-and-turf dinner went down pretty well. After numerous drinks and all the food I could eat, I had about reached my limitations for this night and crawled on off to the room for a much needed sleep. I don't know how long Al stayed with it, but by the way he looked the next morning, I assumed very late.

The next day, Al and I made our way to the airplane carrying our belongings. I had to help him now and then with an extended hand. The weather had gotten very cold and the wet snow had frozen into ice. I knew this would probably cause some problems for takeoff because the airstrip's ruts had frozen as well. I also knew that the airplane would probably be a little hard to start. We got aboard and I prepared to start the engine. I used the normal cold-start procedure by pumping the throttle a few times and then pulled almost all the way back to allow as little air as possible for the fuel mixture, an action that worked fine. It was a severe clear day so that was no problem.

We lined her up on the end of the runway and started the takeoff roll. The plane immediately began to bounce around as a result of the runway ruts. A little past half way down the runway, we just kind of fell into a hole, or so it felt. When the nose of the airplane dropped very low, the propeller hit what I thought was just snow with a "Swoosh." The nose then rose back up, and about that time we lifted off. I heard a swishing noise, and it just didn't feel like the airplane was climbing as well as it should. Nevertheless, I was able to keep on going with no problems, despite the continued noise.

While Al snored away, I flew the airplane back to Knoxville. The swishing persisted, but the plane flew okay even though it didn't have the expected power. After we parked the airplane, we got out to take a closer look. Whatever we hit, the ground or a snow bank or a mound of ice, it bent all three propeller tips back about four inches from the tip, resembling your hand if you folded your outstretched fingers downwards ninety degrees. The propeller-tip bend matched all three blades perfectly. Had just *one* of the three tips broken off, Al and I would have found ourselves in deep doo-doo! As for Al, he didn't appear worried at all. His demeanor, in fact, suggested he simply wanted to go home, to sleep it off, and to call the insurance company the next day.

CHAPTER FIVE
FLYING IN BIAFRA

We now journey into the African-Bush where you will read about a number of really radical aviation experiences that may leave you slack-jawed in amazement. I first learned about the Biafra War in 1968 from a USAF Reserve major who got a ride with our unit on his way home from Biafra to California due to the stoppage of flying because of broken airplanes.

The Nigerian Civil War, known also as the Nigerian-Biafran War, or more commonly as the Biafra War, broke out as a result of the political conflict caused by the attempted secession of the southeastern provinces of Nigeria into the self-proclaimed Republic of Biafra. The war came as a result of economic, ethnic, cultural, and religious tensions among the various people of Nigeria and ran from July 6, 1967, to January 15, 1970, a good year and a half in duration.

The Reserve major informed me of the need of experienced people to restore these busted-up aircraft, handling engine problems for the most part, an aspect of aviation with which I was very familiar, since I had already been working in that field along with my status as flight engineer for the Tennessee Air National Guard. I called the number the major gave me for the company that was involved, namely Flight Test Research of Long Beach, California. This call appeared to be music to the ears of Russell O'Quinn, who was running this endeavor called Joint Church Aid USA.

I accepted the challenge to try to get together a crew to go get this job done. After thinking it all over, I decided on three other comrades who were also in the Tennessee ANG. I knew they were very capable of doing the job that had to be done to get these airplanes going again. They were Ray Boutwell, who came close to getting the crap kicked out of him by actor Robert Mitchum, and twins George and Michael Buero. Of course, we had to get leaves of absence from our unit to be able to accomplish this. I then notified Mr. O'Quinn of having it all together. From there on the ball was in his court.

Soon thereafter we received the plan of action. Ray and the twins hustled off to pick up a C-97 from the Pennsylvania Air National Guard, an aircraft actually in the process of getting sent to the "bone yard" in Arizona. From there they traveled around the USA picking up engines and things needed to restore the airplanes that were already in place at São Tomé Island situated off the West Coast of Africa, where the mission was located. After a few days, I was notified that, while they were flying on their initial leg towards the island, an engine had failed and they were returning to Tennessee to land and try to get the thing fixed. Since this was the exact same type plane that we were already using there in Tennessee, we had parts available to make the repair. We replaced the faulty cylinder that was causing the problem, and away they went.

I was left behind to bring up the rear. I had no visa for my passport, which was required to enter that area, so I had to go through New York, where I was met by a person who provided my passport. He also got me tickets and itinerary for the trip. I flew Pan Am airways from New York to Luanda, Angola, with a stop in Lisbon. This aircraft just happened to be a beautiful Boeing 707. I think the landing in Lisbon was the worst landing I had experienced up to that date, by far one of those panty-hose-down-to-the-ankles landings. When I arrived in Angola, which is Portuguese, I was picked up by a person and delivered to a motel to stay until I could board a flight the next morning to São Tomé.

Biafra was made up of Ibo natives in revolt against Nigeria. We were also there to fly in protein-rich foods and other supplies to this Nigerian enclave, which broke away from Nigeria to form an independent republic. The break was primarily the result of a struggle between the Muslims in the southern region of the country and the Christians in the eastern region (Biafra).

The entire operation on São Tomé rarely averaged over twenty men at one time. Others serving with the program were mostly from a Van Nuys, California, Guard unit. Joint Church Aid began mercy flights into Biafra after the Red Cross was forced to give up the missions early in 1968. The Red Cross lost four crewmen in one flight to the Biafra airstrip when one of its craft was shot down by a Russian-built MIG fighter plane. These fighter planes patrolled the Uli air strip, a converted road, which was Biafra's main link to the outside world. Because of these MIG patrols, relief missions had to be flown at night.

Before the memory slips away into obscurity, Angola's capital, Luanda, at that time was a beautiful city, like something you would see in the movies. The city then turned into an unbelievable mess the next time I was there after the war started in 1975. It was kind of like some areas in Detroit at this time—an abandoned war zone. I was picked up at the motel by the same person who dropped me off there, so I knew I would be safe. He delivered me to the airport and went on his way. The island of São Tomé was also a beautiful place, assuming the appearance you would see in the movies.

The other guys, namely Boutwell and the Buero twins, had already arrived, so the next day we started doing our thing to get the fleet of three planes ready to fly. There they were—three enormous 4-engine C-97 cargo airplanes, with the largest reciprocating engines in the United States hanging on their wings! First, we had to figure a way to get the big monsters off the wings and to set the new ones in position. The Van Nuys ANG personnel who were already in place had a maintenance supervisor. However, after we Tennessee ANG guys arrived, the Van Nuys crew learned right away that we didn't need a supervisor to accomplish what we needed to do. Consequently, the director of operations at that time told us to do our thing and to get some airplanes flying. We went to work right away.

We hired some of the local island guys to help us, mostly for cleaning and things of this nature. One of the guys went by the name Roberto, a little guy who stood about 5' 2" at the most. Could he ever do unbelievably physically demanding things! Ray Boutwell, for instance, was changing a tire on the aircraft one day and had Roberto as his assistant. Ray jokingly told Roberto, who didn't get the joke, he needed him to go get a tire from storage. Ray then proceeded to remove the tire to be replaced off of the gear. At some point, Ray looked up to see Roberto rolling this 300-pound tire like a kid would roll a bicycle tire! Ray and I also discovered in amazement that the locals would wash the airplane with brushes out of buckets filled with raw fuel from the airplane's fuel tanks. Good grief! It's a wonder the whole ramp and everything on it did not blow up! George, one of the Buero twins, came up with a plan that we all thought might work for the engine changes. George took on the job in great stride. He found a shop in the little town that had a large fork lift, which would extend high enough to lift the engines, a feat normally done by a large crane. The only problem was that this engine weighed approximately 6,000 pounds, so George, with his excellent thinking and ingenuity, came up with the plan of placing the same amount of weight ballast on the other end of the fork lift.

Roberto and the 300-pound wheel: "Superman"

We made a WAG (wild-ass guess) regarding the weight and it worked great. It took a couple of days to get the engines changed, and we had to deal with some other things to prepare the big monsters for flight. For example, my crew and I took note of the fact that someone had hit one of the propeller blades on one of the planes, causing substantial damage. We had to improvise a little on this one. So we put our heads together and decided to try cutting about a foot off the damaged prop and then to cut the same amount away from the opposite side prop, an action, we hoped, that should balance them. This worked fine with the exception that this engine would accelerate so much faster that it went into pitch lock. After we got the thing out of pitch lock and made some needed adjustments, the aircraft was good to go. Of course, the engine did not provide as much thrust as before as most of the thrust is produced by the last foot or so at the tip of the prop.

Not only did my crew and I face problems with engines and props, we also discovered a non-operational, rear-cargo-clamshell-cargo door that the local gentlemen could not fix. This door *really* needed to be operational to alleviate the long off-load time at Uli. The longer we had to sit on the ground off-loading, the more the chances increased of getting bombed by the "enemy" that continuously prowled the skies overhead. Mike Buero, a very qualified guy in this field, got the maintenance manual out, reviewed the electrical schematic, jumped right into the middle of the problem, and by the end of the day the door worked well.

Engine Shop on the Ground

Ray Boutwell doing engine repair

The local Portuguese workers got the airplane all loaded and ready to go. The cargo consisted mostly of protein-rich food such as bean, rice, and dried fish. We would launch the aircraft about one hour prior to nightfall in order to arrive at Uli air strip during the cover of darkness because no one wanted to get shot down by the enemy fighters. Uli airstrip was nothing more than a small, asphalt road converted into a runway. The area was surrounded by very tall trees, which couldn't be seen at night, but we found out about their existence later on in the worst kind of way.

Uli's runway-lighting system was lighted with just standard small lights that were powered by a gas-engine generator, which was controllable by the so-called traffic controller somewhere on the ground. We were never there in daylight, so we knew nothing about what the place looked like. All the messages from aircraft to controller were in code to prevent anyone else to know who we were or the arrival time. All the approaches were the very basic automatic directional finder (ADF) approaches, which were very difficult because they only got you to the area of the runway. This is what you might consider a pilot's *real* seat-of-the-pants flying. I would venture to say that there would be very few pilots flying the major airlines' highly sophisticated aircraft of today who would believe this alien-aviation environment. It's really a different world. I have been there and have done both.

I wasn't initially hired to go to this volatile "theater" as a pilot. We, that is to say, Ray and the twins, were hired to get the aircraft ready to fly and to perform flight-engineer duties. It was known that I had all my licenses, including a pilot license. I had also flown the KC-97 some while flying with the Air National Guard. In addition, I had observed pilots for so long in all kinds of adverse conditions and emergencies that I was very familiar with many aspects of flying an airplane.

Once we had successfully launched a few flights, one of the maintenance guys awakened me one night with the news that Jim Andrew wanted me to come promptly to the airport. In the belief that something serious had taken place, I dressed and scurried off to see Mr. Andrew.

At first, I thought they were having an engine problem, and I was the one most familiar with engines. It came to me as surprise—and a pleasant one at that—when Jim asked me if I thought I could fill the position of an absent copilot. Jim said he had to fire the one he had and needed me to fill in until one of the other copilots returned from leave. I grabbed my butt, threw it into the right seat, and three of us went!

Jim handed me the communications code book to review on the way. After we got the cruising altitude leveled off, I asked him what happened with the other guy. Jim said that the copilot *almost* caused him to land gear up. For some reason, the copilot raised the landing gear right before touchdown, and Jim had to make a quick go around, almost not making it. Needless to say, that was the end of this guy's flying with Jim Andrew.

I continued flying as Jim's copilot until the other copilot returned, but I guess after all the things that happened to us in the meantime, such as getting in the trees and things like that, Jim concluded that I would be his permanent copilot, a position which suited me just fine. I guess Jim, George, and I just kind of grew on each other. I could not have asked for a better crew. We would even pour down a cold beer on the last trip home every night.

 Needless to say, there were no flight attendants or martinis on board. These flights were all made under very adverse conditions, including the continuous problem of ground fire whenever we approached the airport. And the fact that we were always in total darkness with very limited approach-guidance equipment, such as an instrument landing system (ILS) or VHF Omni-directional radio range (VOR) approach, made these flights even more life threatening. The only approach available was the automatic direction finder (ADF), virtually nothing more than a radio transmission, or beacon between the aircraft and a suitable radio station.

After a few flights of sitting two to three hours in the airplane waiting for the Ibos to off-load the aircraft, bombs splitting the ground all around us, we decided we needed to decrease this dangerous condition. Thanks to George, we devised and constructed a pallet and roller system to work inside the airplane. He found some rollers like the ones used in tractor-trailer trucks to move cargo. He came back with enough of these rollers to install along the cargo floor. The tie-down loops were already there since this was a cargo airplane. George also figured out a way to tie these rollers in place. He then purchased some 4' x 8' x 1' plywood panels from the local boat yard and installed hooks and cables on the plywood so that we could hook the pallet to the existing monorail located on the ceiling of the airplane. With this system now in place, we could push the pallet of cargo out the rear of the airplane, retrieve the pallet, and store it along the side walls—all in all, a very workable system, reducing our off-load time probably by a couple of hours. Was this great ingenuity or what?

We experienced another significant problem: finding the runway, especially in bad weather and coordinating with the controller when to turn the runway lights on. If he turned them on too soon, there was always the danger of the other side's ground fire. On the other side of the coin, if he turned them on too late, we would miss sight of the runway.

On one occasion, when we had difficulty finding the runway for a drop, I thought all of us would soon buy the farm. On our first pass in total darkness and in lingering fog clear down to the tree tops, we were unable to get low enough to see the runway for landing. So we went around for another try. The weather was really bad this particular night. The runway was hard enough to find anyway, and, when the weather was bad, it was virtually impossible to locate.

Jim Andrew, functioning as captain on this delivery, decided to try going just that little bit lower. All of a sudden, with a big "bang" or two (perhaps more!) and the screeching of the tree limbs across the airplane as we hit the trees, we knew we had big problems. The airplane yawed very badly, almost ejecting the engineer, George Buero, from his seat. George finally got the power up to full power as requested by the captain for go around. Once we had composed ourselves from the sudden panic, we did our normal go-around procedure, at the same time praying that we could get this thing around again and on the ground.

We finally gathered ourselves together, cleaned our pants, and decided to try to get this thing landed, not knowing what damage we had or if we could make it back to the airport. We succeeded, and I am here to tell about it.

Captain Jim exited the airplane to check the damage. When he returned, I noticed he was very white looking in the face. He said that the wing tips and leading edge were damaged pretty badly, but the Ibos had already removed the tree limbs from the wings, flaps, landing gear, and other places. But now he wanted *me* to fly the return trip. I did as he asked. Everything appeared to be working fine except for the operation of the ailerons. When passing the center point, the right one would stick because the wing-tip cone was bent into the aileron and took some pressure to move it past that point. Fortunately for us, we got the aircraft back without any further problems.

After we got back and landed the airplane, we all took another look at the damage. What really got our attention was that the cone at the wing tip was flat against the wing spar, indicating that one more inch closer and the spar would have contacted the tree trunk. That *one single inch* meant that we would probably not have been here to tell this story. Even to this day, I experience nightmarish dreams about that particular incident.

George (left) , Me (center), and Captain Jim at São Tomé

Me and George

Too Close for Comfort

We did have an out-of-service airplane though that needed wing tips, which we dismantled from another C-97 that landed gear up by Red Cross pilots who had flown missions prior to our arrival. We located a few volunteer maintenance people who flew along with us, carrying their tools and equipment to the Uli airstrip. These folks removed the leading edges, wing tips, and other parts to repair our damaged airplane. I think that was the first time anyone of our people had been to Uli in the daytime. We picked them up on our next off-loading flight. The flying continued in the same manner at night and fixing the mechanical problems during the day. Our maintenance facility was very non-standard, with the engine shop outside and with engines lying on the ground. It was one of those things when you just make it work by skill, by cunning, and by perseverance.

You have to picture this area as a war zone, as it was. The people there were starving, which is the main reason we were there in the first place. They were starving so bad that it wasn't unusual for one of them to steal food supplies to feed their families. Armed soldiers guarded the off-load operation. Occasionally we would hear the "rat, tat, tat" of rifle fire, which spewed forth from the AK-47s issued to them. We knew that someone had grabbed a sack of beans or something and had tried to flee with stolen food. At times, the AK-47 shells hit their intended target: we would observe someone dragging the body to a truck to be hauled away.

One food thief wound up paying dearly for his act. An Ibo grabbed a bag of beans and sprinted away with it. Forgetting that we always left at least one engine running during off-load to be able to start the other ones when ready to shove off, the poor fellow ran directly into the big propeller, which severed both his arms up to the elbow. Nonetheless, the pilfering took place on virtually every trip. We don't really know how many other people, whether thieves or not, were hit by the aircraft propellers. I do recall the time we found a hat in the carburetor intake when trying to find the reason for the roughly running engine. We wrote about the discrepancy in the aircraft manual. The next day it was signed off as follows in the correction box: "Part of Ibo removed from carburetor intake."

The other pilots who were already there before we arrived to repair the aircraft seemed simply to behave as though they were vacationing. Then, too, they all had a strange variety of names: Bat Masterson, Johnny Cash, Jack Frost, and Peter Knox. I was known as "Moon" Mullins to most people, which I didn't care too much to hear because it was a common name of several others in the little town in which I grew up.

Life on the Beautiful Tropical Island of *São Tomé*

São Tomé lies 125 miles from the Western Coast of Africa. It is a province of Portugal, lying in the Gulf of Guinea, itself about fifteen miles from the equator. Housing—small, stucco dwellings constructed without windows—therefore, had to be built to conform to the steaming, tropical climate. Although the dwellings helped moderate the heat, they lacked the luxuries of the American home, particularly hot, running water. The women washed the family clothes in the river, which ran through the island, and ironed them with hollow, metal irons heated with live coals, which reminded me of the old days growing up in West Virginia. Accustomed to home-cooked, American-style meals, we found São Tomé's native dishes, all cooked in a bath of palm oil, more than just a little hard to swallow.

Washy-Washy on the River

However, with a little Southern America ingenuity, Ray Boutwell introduced a few staples to the diet of the natives: hamburgers, black-eyed peas, barbecued beef, chicken, and even banana splits. In fact, this type of cooking became a common thing at our house of residence. As keenly as Ray managed foresight over the ins and outs of aviation, my buddy Ray, who came close to a fistfight with none other than Robert Mitchum a number of years earlier, kept at least a pot of beans and a pone of corn bread always available for any of our personnel anytime they desired a good American-cooked meal. We would also prepare barbeques at our residence and invite any interested locals in the neighborhood to participate with us.

Toting the clothes to the Casa

This little island, actually an Africa-in-miniature form, sparkled with a fabulous diversity of dramatic scenery, exotic birds, luxuriant foliage, and beautiful waterfalls, all framed naturally by beautifully golden beaches. When we were there in 1969, the island was occupied mostly by the local natives and some Portuguese. We were virtually the only Americans present.

Naturally, since boys will forever be boys, there would always be a need for a place to gather for wine, women, and recreation, except for me, of course. At the time, the island sported one and only one hotel, the Hotel Miramar. In truth, the majority of our personnel resided there already. Located directly on a beautiful beach where lots of lovely local women were always bathing in the tropical sun, the hotel created the atmosphere for our gathering place. Naturally, I was not really *that* interested; I just went there to be with my other comrades. No kidding. Ha!

Some of the pilots brought their wives or girlfriends to the island. Some of the ladies would even accompany the flyboys on their off-loading missions! We had one particular pilot who would let his girlfriend talk to the controllers, giving the coded information for the arrival time as well as other information. As you may now surmise, this was indeed a very loosely run operation.

At one point, we found ourselves in need of parts to keep the operation going. The closest place to acquire the necessary parts was at Tel Aviv in Israel. With his intelligence and great personality, Ray Boutwell was the man for this job. There was no doubt that he could handle the negotiations there with the overhaul company to acquire the parts. I think we even ended up buying an engine or two from them, a purchase that proved to be very reliable. I have no reservations about saying that I don't believe a group of guys could have been found anywhere that could even come close to the performance of these guys.

Now it was vacation time. So back to Tennessee I went, but not before an invitation to visit the company's office in California. I had no idea why this was necessary, but it was fine with me, because I could pick up my pay that had accumulated for the past tour. Except for living expenses, we received no pay during our months transporting goods to Biafra. I called my wife and asked her if she would like to meet me in Atlanta to accompany me on my way to California. She agreed. We hooked up in Atlanta and ventured on to California, flying the friendly skies of United. It seemed abnormal to fly around the country without getting shot at.

We arrived at the Flight Test Research office and met with the people for whom I had been working but had never met personally. As I expected, they were pretty fine people. After talking to Mr. O'Quinn for a while about the operation, I finally found out the reason he invited me to come to the office: he wanted me to consider returning to the island as director of operations, an offer that came as a surprise. I told him that I was humbled by the offer but would have to think it over during my time at home. Evidently, some of the guys from the Van Nuys ANG unit recommended me for the position.

My wife had been experiencing health problems all the time I was gone. We had this little farm that she had to take care of by herself, and it was kind of taking its toll on her. Because her health continued to deteriorate, I decided not to accept Mr. O'Quinn's position. In the meantime, Ray Boutwell had also returned home at the same time. I finally recommended his name to assume the position on the island, and Ray did accept. As for me, I didn't return to São Tomé until several years later, and I promise to talk about that adventure in a later section of this book.

It wasn't too long after that when the crewmembers to which this book is dedicated were all killed by flying too low and hitting the trees as we did. Regrettably, they weren't as lucky as we were. I was at home on vacation when the crash happened. I got the information from a friend who gave me a newspaper clipping of the accident

CHAPTER SIX

"CALIFORNIA VACATION IS OVER"

Back to TANG

I resumed my position with the Tennessee Air National Guard (TANG) as a civil service technician. We continued flying the KC-97 refueling tankers in the US and Europe, with some deployments to Canada and Alaska. The Europe operation was called "Creek Party," which was handled by the Air National refueling units in several states in the USA. It was a rotational thing with each unit doing a month at a time. I enjoyed the European flying very much and stayed there as much as I could, because all active duty time would add to my retirement pay if I ever made it to that point.

At the same time, I was still doing my part-time flying and instructing at the other side of the airport. I still reserved the thought in my mind of one day flying the beautiful Boeing 707. Furthermore, I managed to chalk up great flying experiences by watching every move the pilots made. These guys were all veterans of previous flying in the USAF, with positions now in all walks of life, such as airline pilots, lawyers, doctors, and even one chicken farmer. Nevertheless, when it came to flying, I would rate them second to none. I learned a lot just watching how they handled the aircraft in normal conditions as well as during adverse conditions, such as bad weather and emergency situations. The in-flight refueling business included lots of bad variables. These guys were proven professionals in every aspect of life. I was very fortunate to have been able to fly with them.

One aircraft commander I really enjoyed flying with was Major Bob Worrell. This guy was a natural pilot if I ever saw one. No matter how bad of a situation we would get into, he would never appear to be shaken in the least. I never saw him sweat. We were flying into Bermuda Naval Air Station one time. The cross-wind was the worst I had ever seen. It was so bad that it looked like we were approaching the runway sideways. Major Worrell just kept flying the big KC-97 like there was nothing to it, but to me, well, I sweated it out all the way down, on occasion rising out of my seat, curious to see if we were going to get this thing on the ground or not.

Right before we touched the ground, Major Worrell dropped the right wing down, straightening the aircraft to the runway at the same time, and made a beautiful grease-job landing. He never said anything, and, when we were on the crew bus, I mentioned to him something about the cross wind. With an ear-to-ear smile, he asked, "What cross wind?" He was a cool dude. Of course, as I mentioned before, all the guys were excellent pilots. They were the types of pilots who would never let you see them sweat. I have always tried to program myself to those guys. They were also the same guys who flew the F-104 aircraft when we deployed to Germany during the Berlin Crisis, setting numerous flying records.

In about 1978 the Tennessee ANG switched from KC-97 to KC-135 aircraft, neither requiring a flight engineer. At that time, I transferred to a unit at Charleston AFB, South Carolina, which operated C-141 cargo carriers. With this unit, I picked up lots of traveling experience to many foreign countries. This was a big, slow-moving jet, which carried a lot of cargo and troops. We operated all over the world to all military bases: Air Force, Navy, Army, and civilian. We would stay out for a week or two at a time.

On one trip, we landed at Rhein Main Air Base in West Germany, known then as the military "Gateway to Europe." The "Gateway," by the way, closed its U.S. military operations officially on October 1, 2005. Once we had landed, we noticed a broken Air Force C-141 that had been transporting people out of Tehran. One of their flight engineers, we learned, had gotten sick. Because we maintained three on our aircraft, one of us had to go with the Air Force crew to take his place. We flipped a coin to determine who would join up with them. I lost the flip and accompanied the new crew. We were placed on standby at the on-base hotel for about a week waiting for the aircraft to be repaired. We were officially on standby until 6 pm. After that we were free to do whatever we wanted. Needless to say, we enjoyed ourselves because the hotel had a nice bar, cold beer, and lots of hot-and-cold-running women. Occasionally, we would just enjoy a friendly poker game.

CHAPTER SEVEN
"THE ARIZONA DESERT"

Bangladesh Adventure

After a couple of years, most likely now in the 1970s, the same guys as before were called upon by Mr. O'Quinn to help him in another life-support mission called Foundation for Airborne Relief (FAR) in Bangladesh. To be able to accomplish this feat, we first had to acquire the aircraft. I think a deal was made between Mr. O'Quinn and the U.S. Government to collect some C-133 aircraft out of the bone yard located at Davis-Monthan AFB near Tucson, Arizona.

According to my best recollection, it must have been in July of 1972 when we all gathered at the bone yard. This place was filled with perhaps thousands of moth-balled aircraft. You wouldn't believe your eyes unless you were there to actually see this place. It looked as though every aircraft in the world had been parked there. They were all lined up like a squadron of soldiers in a marching parade. Almost everything that the military has ever used was there, literally miles and miles of stored aircraft from all branches of the military. Aside from inert frames of aircraft, the place also served as haven for all kinds of desert life, including snakes, lizards, and almost everything that either slithered or crawled in a desert. The aircraft made terrific homes for them.

I had already been to the bone yard several times before delivering the KC-97s when the ANG was changing to KC-135s. But I had never spent any time there working to get airplanes repaired and operational to be able to fly them again! We could see right away that this task was going to be *almost* too hard to accomplish. On the other side of the coin, the idea of quitting when faced with challenges still did not occupy our heads. So off we went again with the skill, the cunning, and the perseverance we had shown earlier in Biafra to get the job done.

This task would require lots of assistance from the maintenance people who were stationed there. We found them very willing to help us any way they could. The main thing that we were in need of was heavy equipment, like jacks and lifts to move heavy things such as engines and things of that nature. The aircraft lay virtually on the ground, with flat tires and struts digging into the earth.

The weather conditions and the working conditions in the middle of the desert during summer months can only be described as horrible. Temperatures remained well above 100 degrees. We worked for the most part outside in the hot sun. Our only shade was either under the plane or in it. To get in the cool for a while, we would have to walk about a mile to the maintenance building, which wasn't worth it. Of course, at that time the greater majority of us were young and full of piss and vinegar. I think most of us would also swig enough booze during the night to keep us kind of numb through the day anyway—that was, of course, when Mr. O'Quinn wasn't around because I was told he was a Baptist preacher.

After I was there for what seemed an unimaginable amount of time, I received word to go to Long Beach, California. The company wanted me to take a look at another planned project. Without hesitation, I grabbed my bag and hauled my butt to Long Beach, California. I first went to Mr. O'Quinn's office for a while. We primarily discussed Biafra and the project we were on now at the bone yard. Then he sent me off to see another fellow in charge of the project that Mr. O'Quinn wanted me to consider.

I met the man, who informed me that the company had acquired an old Aero Commander through donation from a company in Alaska. Mr. O'Quinn remembered my performance in Biafra and told the guy that I could probably do it if anyone could. I could tell by talking to this guy that he knew about as much about airplanes as I did about being a preacher.

In short, if I accepted the project, I would have to go to Alaska to pick up the aircraft and fly it to Long Beach, the company's base of operations. Anyway, to satisfy him, I told him that I would check it out and let him know if I thought I could possibly do the job. By telephone connection, I contacted the person who knew something about the Aero Commander. Right off the bat, he started laughing at the idea that I would actually attempt to fly the aircraft down to Long Beach, explaining all the problems with the airplane. I could see right away that this project probably wasn't going anywhere, and I subsequently turned down the proposal.

I reported my findings to the gentleman to whom Mr. O'Quinn had sent me at the beginning of all this nonsense. I got the feeling that he, the gentleman, thought I was just blowing smoke and didn't want to go get the airplane. This was, of course, not true. I saw right away that it was useless to discuss it with him any further, so I went to Mr. O'Quinn, explaining the problems with the aircraft to him and the enormous estimated costs that we would encounter. Mr. O'Quinn understood what I was saying and the case was closed. I suspected the other guy may have already mentioned some bad words about me to Mr. O'Quinn, but Mr. O'Quinn knew me better as a result of my own contribution to support his earlier Biafra mission. One had to respect a person like Mr. O'Quinn for his continuing efforts to help people in need.

So after that little fiasco, I journeyed back to the desert. I arrived, I think, on a Friday, just before the weekend fun began. We did take off most the weekends, loading up the vehicles with lots of cold beverages and steaks to barbeque, including other requirements for recreation, such as some of the local girls who had arrived for some recreational fun in the mountains.

For some reason, this operation was then put on the table. Most of us went back to our previous activities. I think George Buero stayed with the operation until they finally got one airplane operational enough to move it to the Mojave Airport in the desert. I then heard that the operation was completely closed down.

CHAPTER EIGHT
FINALLY! AIRLINE EMPLOYMENT!

While flying with the unit at Charleston in 1978, I met a fellow engineer named Bill Brantley, who was flying for a cargo carrier in Miami called Fleming Airways. He informed me that the company needed flight crews at the time, so I decided to check it out. I called the company and spoke with Chief Flight Engineer Roy Harrison, a retired Air Force flight engineer. "Come on down!" he said, further noting I'd be welcome to join a new class starting in a couple of weeks. I made a couple more trips out of Charleston, went home, gathered up some things for the stay, and headed for Miami.

Roy Harrison impressed me greatly with his knowledge of aircraft, especially the Lockheed Electra, the aircraft we would use for training. Roy hailed from Oklahoma and I came from Tennessee; consequently, we hit it off right away, I guess, if only because we talked the same southern drawl. I first stayed in a motel. Roy lived alone in an apartment building south of Miami. He was kind enough to invite me to stay with him while in training. I took him up on that, saving a bunch of money for one thing. He also helped my progress in the school, considering the total amount of time I would spend with him, the classroom instructor. What a deal!

It was pretty evident why the aircraft on which we trained was called the Electra: everything on board appeared to operate electrically. As Roy said, "If you can learn the electrical system, you will know the airplane," words I found to be true. Roy proved to be probably the best instructor I had ever met. He knew this airplane inside and out and kept the class in an uproar all the time with his antics, his manner of speech, and his expressions. There was never a dull day in his classroom.

One classroom buddy I befriended was Jim Daniels, an ex-Eastern pilot who had been in a DC-9 crash on approach in North Carolina about five years earlier. For Jim, the flight-engineer position represented his way to get back into aviation. As for me, the position would eventually allow me to get my foot in the door for a pilot upgrade later on.

Jim had been in and out of the hospital over the past five years and had just gotten his medical back. *Final Approach: The Crash of Eastern 212* written by William Stockton, recounts the mishap and makes for an interesting read, in my view.

After the ground school and simulator training in Miami on the famous 36th street, Jim and I loaded up and headed for Ypsilanti, Michigan, to begin initial flight training, to take the FAA required turbo prop-flight engineer exam, and to prepare ourselves for the aircraft check ride.

We made it through all the hoops and were ready to fly and to make some money. This old airport at Ypsilanti had been there since World War II, serving then as assembly plant of the B-24 bomber. In fact, one of the bombers still perched there at the airport. I remember the parking ramp most of all, a nasty thing so coated with oil that it was difficult to walk on let alone taxi an airplane full of cargo, almost like skating on ice after a rainfall.

The airport had everything from Twin Beach aircraft to DC-8s operating out of there at that time, creating a level of chaos that had to be seen to be believed. It was not uncommon for someone occasionally to bang a wing or to hit a tug. The airport also served as a central, auto-parts shipping terminal, shipping automotive parts to plants all over the United States—non-skedding at its finest.

The Electra aircraft we flew were old passenger planes that had been converted into cargo-carrier airplanes. I think the Electra was the most forgiving airplane I ever flew. The thing had so much power that it would actually fly with one engine, providing it was not loaded with cargo. It was a stiff-flying machine because the wings held the fuel cells. Years later in Angola, we flew one that had a crack so big in the top of the wing that you could see the fuel in the tank, an account discussed later in the section on Angola.

These people at Ypsilanti were obviously in this business to make money, not to make people comfortable. The airplanes were maintained just enough to get by the FAA checks and sometimes not that well. Most of the crews flying these things were professionals on how to keep them going. They, too, were in it for the money—"no fly, no pay." Their main concern concentrated on making sure that the minimum equipment list (MEL) was available and filled out properly.

It was not unusual to fly without operational radar, with a required radio that was not working, or even with an oil leak in an engine that would be shut down after takeoff and restarted prior to landing so no one would see it. We would also fly the aircraft with a propeller oil leak. We would continue operating it until the propeller RPMs would start fluctuating. When the fluctuation got too bad, we would just shut it down until the next approach and then restart for landing. We'd service it on the ground and go again as though nothing had happened.

The best thing you had going for you in this business was to know the aircraft systems well enough to be able to improvise and to keep the thing going. To reiterate Roy Harrison's words, "If you know the electrical system, you know the airplane," because everything was controlled by relays. I remember one time when an "Ace" (noted sarcastically) from the base landed the airplane so hard going into Atlanta that it opened all the relays, cutting off all the power. We bounced up and down in total darkness. Then all of a sudden the electrical system started coming back on, one relay at a time, until power was restored.

Air-Start Door Malfunction

Flying the Electra, we learned, seemed continuously to provide certain unanticipated opportunities for reaction. One day, for instance, the maintenance guys left the air start located on the right wing unfastened. After takeoff we all felt a heaviness that prompted us to make a steeper angle of attack to get the airplane to fly. All of a sudden, we started getting this violent vibration. We couldn't figure out what it was or how to stop it. We had the loadmaster check around outside to see if he could see anything. He came back up to the cockpit and said the air-start door had risen up at the wing. We didn't know what to do, and we didn't want to have to go back to land. Besides, we were too heavy to make a safe landing for one thing, and we didn't want to dump any of the costly fuel. With some thoughtful effort, we remembered that the problem didn't begin until we raised the nose up. We figured if we put the nose back down into a steep descent, the action might blow the door closed. We put the nose down a little and nothing happened. We decided to try it with one big push forward for just a second. When we did it that time, everything smoothed out seemingly in an instant. Needless to say, from that time on we personally checked to make sure that door was closed prior to each flight. I think most everyone who flies the Electra today does the same.

Loose Barrels in the Mythical Bermuda Triangle

Sometime during the early part of 1978, I recall one time when we were contracted by a company to pick up a load of fire-depressant material at Logan Airport in Boston for transport to Bermuda. A tanker ship had an oil spill that went ablaze and fire crews couldn't put it out.

The work crew loaded this stuff onto the airplane in 55-gallon barrels and tied them down with rope, which didn't appear to me to be sufficient, but no one said anything. Captain Lee was busy doing his instructing with the student pilot. I think we were a little overweight as usual for takeoff. It looked like we were going to have a good day for flying, and the weather forecast reported no problems.

Those pilots who have flown through the Bermuda Triangle know well how things can change at the snap of the fingers. We were flying along just fat, dumb, and happy until we came upon a cloud layer. Because the layer bumped us around somewhat, Capt. Lee decided to climb the airplane to a higher altitude. I advised him of our weight and that we were too heavy for that altitude.

Going against my advice, he began to put the aircraft into a climb. When the airplane wasn't climbing at its normal rate, he asked for some more power. I told him we were already at max power. In truth, we had slowed considerably, and the airplane started shaking violently so much that all hell broke loose in the back: the barrels had dislodged themselves and were rolling everywhere. The nose would go down and the barrels would roll to the front; the nose would go up and they would roll to the rear. It was kind of like being on a roller coaster.

Captain Lee finally got the oscillation under control and put the nose down into a very slow descent. He said he would hold the airplane in that position while the copilot and I went back to try to get the barrels arranged so that the airplane would fly normally. We placed the barrels where we thought they would be balanced well enough to fly. Some of the barrels had wedged themselves at the rear of the airplane and couldn't be repositioned, so we secured them as best we could with rope. We set a number of other barrels upright so they wouldn't roll anymore and tied down them as best we could.

This was not an easy task because these barrels probably weighed some 400 pounds each. I guess when you get the "doo-doo" scared out of you, you become a physically stronger person. Besides, what we did was really not the safest thing to attempt. If we had happened to hit more turbulence, it could easily have meant "Katie bar the door" (there's trouble ahead!) for us. The copilot and I then returned to the cockpit to determine how the captain was doing flying the plane. He indicated he had things under control, but he didn't know what to expect when we slowed for landing. Very soon we would find out, bringing to mind that all of this occurred within the Bermuda Triangle.

We continued toward our destination, not knowing what to expect on approach and landing. All was going very well until we got on the approach and had to slow the aircraft. At that time, Captain Lee concluded that the airplane was more tail heavy now than he had realized. We had already anticipated the heavier weight in the rear as a result of the barrels that we could not reposition.

He had to keep the airspeed way above the normal approach speed to the ground. He did a really good job of it. The airplane was so tail heavy that he had to taxi with the power increased and to ride the brakes to keep us from falling on our butt. He also had to continue holding the power up after stopping in the parking spot while I, the engineer, scooted outside to install the tail stand before we could shut the engines down. After that it was time to go to the motel, to change our pants again, and to make a beeline to the bar to put down a "jar."

This near-death fiasco demanded several jars to unwind. We just wanted to get away from that airplane for a while.

We finally decided to go back the airplane to check for damage. When we arrived, we noticed fuel all over the ramp under the airplane. We figured the stall, along with the barrels rolling back and forth in the plane, caused a fuel leak in the wing (the wing on this airplane is a fuel tank). After further review, we discovered that there was a crack where the wing attached to the fuselage. Needless to say, we were not going anywhere for a while. We contacted the company about the problem, which put the ball in their hands. So again we made the very important decision to go back to the bar for a few more jars until further notice from the company. To the best of my memory, we also headed for the beach to check out the activity there, a setting that would be far better than inhaling the fuel on the ramp. Oh, by the way, we did hear that the fire crew finally suppressed the fire on the tanker. At least it wasn't a wasted day.

"Oops!" No Ailerons!

As we knew, this operation totally differed from a scheduled airline. To be able to make some money, we had to place ourselves within reach of the airplane, hoping for a trip to haul cargo. After sitting standby in Miami for a week early in 1978, the call finally came. Miami was also the company's maintenance station. The mechanics were young and inexperienced. The call came for a trip to Willow Run Airport in Ypsilanti, Michigan, to pick up auto parts to deliver to Buffalo, New York. After arriving at the maintenance ramp to pick up the airplane, it was found that the airplane was still undergoing flight readiness. Finally, the maintenance crew had it ready to go, assuring that everything had been checked. The aircraft was boarded, the normal checklist was completed, and the flight was on its way.

According to the weather report, "severe clear" weather would be experienced for the night flying. The aircraft was lined up and started the takeoff roll. Everything appeared to be normal—V1, rotate. Right after rotation, when it is necessary to fly the airplane with the normal controls, the work of the novice maintenance crew came into play: there was no movement of the ailerons—yes, that is what I said. The ailerons were not moving.

Captain Bill, the aircraft's pilot, turned the wheel left and right, but no response. At the same time, the airplane veered to the right into an un-controllable right turn and headed toward the control tower. The copilot's seat had physically slipped to the full-aft position, so he was out of the picture for a little while, but this particular captain was a very good pilot. He knew enough to realize he had other ways of straightening out this airplane to prevent crashing into the tower or something worse.

His action was immediate, and without hesitation he used asymmetrical engine power control along with the rudder to level the airplane, which sent it flying straight again but still in a slight climb. The copilot, in the meantime, had finally readjusted his seat to the normal position to help fly the plane. Captain Bill checked to see if everyone was still with him and doing okay. There was really nothing anyone but Captain Bill could do at the time except to sit there and get an education on how to fly an airplane with no aileron control.

His next problem was getting this thing back on the ground. He knew the airplane was too heavy to make a safe landing, especially under those conditions, so he decided to fly around for a while. This would burn some fuel and at the same time give him practice flying the airplane with no aileron control. After about forty-five minutes or so, he decided it was time to try to get this thing on the ground. He had the tower vector him around on a long turn to line him up with the runway for about a ten-mile final. There was virtually no wind this night, which made things much easier. With a strong crosswind blowing, it would probably not be possible to land the airplane with no aileron control.

I guess the good Lord was looking down on the crew. Once the captain got the aircraft lined up and connected to the ILS, it appeared that he had it under control. He kept the airplane perfectly on the ILS approach by making very small corrections, knowing, if he got off course, it would be very hard to get back. He was making a better approach than you see some people do with everything working. He flew the airplane all the way down the glide slope perfectly and made the best landing he had experienced in a long time. He could see the guys manning the fire trucks and emergency equipment clapping their hands as he taxied clear of the runway.

After Captain Bill got back to the parking area and had maintenance check it out, the finding was that they had left the ailerons disconnected after working on a different system that required them to be disconnected. I think there were a couple less maintenance workers the next day. This incident must have cost the company a pile of money as that emergency equipment doesn't come cheap.

Loose Engine and Hole in Fuselage

One day in 1979 we were called for a trip to transport automobile engines to the plant in Buffalo, New York. It was another beautiful, clear day with no expectations of any problems. We just rode along—fat, dumb, and happy—opened up a couple of cans of Kipper snacks and saltines, which was our normal caliber of non-gourmet meals for these flights, food only slightly better than military C-rations. Sometimes we would splurge and put down some Vienna sausages. Of course, we had no flight attendants or passengers in the back to bitch about the smell, which believe me, created a reek throughout the airplane.

We all now had full bellies, so we just laid back and relaxed until it was time for our descent into Buffalo. The night was so clear we could see the airport from at least thirty miles away. It should not have been any problem at all to get the airplane down today. But for some reason, there must have been an unusual amount of traffic that day, and the controller had to put the arrivals in a short holding pattern to be able to get us all in safely.

Finally, it was our turn to begin the approach. The controller gave us a vector to the final approach course but forgot to give us a lower altitude. Captain Bill didn't say anything about a lower altitude and neither did the controller. When he finally gave us the clearance to land, we were too high to get down for a safe landing from that point. Ace, I mean Captain Bill, decided to go ahead with the approach and put the airplane in a slip maneuver to get it down, which is not really a big problem with an empty airplane but not recommended with a load of cargo on board—especially those heavy engines.

So Captain Bill proceeded with his fantastic aerobatic maneuver anyway. As soon as he put the airplane into the slip, one of the aircraft engines came loose. We next took note of the engine breaking apart from its mounts and smashing into the left side of the airplane. Because our ears began to pop, we knew we had suddenly lost cabin pressure, but at that altitude it wasn't a big problem. You can imagine what would have happened if we were at a high altitude. Everything in sight small enough to go through the hole would go there immediately. The big problem was the big hole in the side of the airplane, with part of the engine sticking out. As we well knew, these types of incidents never set well with the company president, since we would now be without an airplane to fly, and our only source of revenue production would be grounded. We were almost certain that he, Captain Bill, had a sore butt for a few days after the chewing.

Damaged, Out-of-Control Starter

In 1979 an incident happened while doing Log-Air contracts for the USAF. Our normal flight schedule for the day was to leave Warner-Robins AFB in Georgia, to fly to Shaw AFB, South Carolina, to Langley AFB, Virginia, to Charleston AFB, South Carolina, and then to return to Warner Robins to rest until the next morning. At 11:00 a.m. the next morning, we would fly the same route again. Everything went very well during the first leg to Shaw and the second leg to Langley. After the off load was completed at Langley and we were starting engines, the #2 and #1 engines started without any problem. When we tried to start the #3 engine, everything was going fine until the starter appeared to have disengaged from the engine, and we heard the unusually very loud sound of the starter over-speeding until it blew completely apart, coming through parts of the engine cowling, with one section of the cowling leaving the airplane completely. This was a very dangerous situation because, when this thing blows, it goes everywhere. It could even possibly come through the fuselage and into the cockpit or cabin and do serious damage to anything inside, which could be passengers.

There is a safety switch incorporated with this type of starter to prevent this from happening in the event it starts to over speed. This switch will turn on a red warning light in the cockpit, which is observed during starts that will give the flight engineer plenty time to terminate the start if this occurs. As I mentioned earlier, the maintenance was never up to par in this kind of business. So it was found out after it all happened that this safety light was coming on and staying illuminated at times when there was no problem—the basic false indication. So the maintenance fix for the problem was simply to disconnect the wiring to the switch to disable the light. What was possibly one of the most important safety features on the airplane was disabled by maintenance to avoid having to trouble shoot it and to repair it properly. The world of non-sked flying is fraught with pitfalls of this nature on a regular basis. Most non-sked operators are frequently cutting corners on maintenance to reduce their operating costs.

Dynamite to Vienna, Austria

Finally, I experienced a potentially explosive trip on the Electra with Captain Lee and a crewmember named Ray Fiend—both excellent, reliable pilots—to deliver a load of dynamite and caps to Vienna, Austria. We were to pick up the goods and the Electra out of Goose Bay, Labrador, and to deliver to Vienna. We flew to Goose Bay by commercial airline. The Electra, so we heard, was supposed to be in tip-top shape, but we know what this can mean, right? The navigation system consisted of the now dinosaur-aged Loran radio, a system that existed long before we had all the good stuff in today's GPS and satellites, communications technology that has greatly improved the art of navigation.

We took on just about all that the Electra would be capable to carry—plus a little extra, as usual. We then began to make our way across the North Atlantic. Our route would take us just south of the tip of Greenland, over England, and finally to Vienna. We were doing just fine until the Loran set went tits up, as usual, resulting in my first observation on how to cross the Atlantic without proper navigation aids. Ace would have to navigate by using the ADF beacons to get a cross reference for the crossing points at least close to our coordinates. I don't remember which beacons he used, but it worked out okay, for we made it without any incidents.

However, one problem almost always tends to lead to another problem. When Ray pulled out the European charts, we saw they were so far outdated that we didn't know if they could be used. After Captain Lee tried a few of the VOR frequencies (not operational for the most part) that were on the charts, he did a smart thing in my opinion: telling controllers that something had spilled on the charts and that he was unable to read the numbers. Thanks to the verbal help of the controllers, we did make it the rest of the way to Vienna with Captain Lee's "new" system.

It is very seldom, if ever at all, that European controllers give you a direct to another distant VOR to make it easier to navigate. Normally, they clear you to one fix at a time and not clear you to the next one until you are almost on top of the one toward which you are navigating, certainly an episode more than a little different than flying in the U.S.A.

Anyway, we did make it to Vienna without blowing ourselves out of the sky. I didn't really know if hauling dynamite in airplanes was a standard thing or not, but it paid money, so it was okay with me. Besides, the guys unloading this stuff didn't appear to show any hesitation or fear at all when I considered they tossed and stacked everything as though unloading bales of hay from a farmer's wagon. On the other hand, I could not avoid the vivid image of the Electra bursting into thousands of pieces had we had encountered severe weather with the chance of lightning strikes. Yes, this was my first adventure crossing the Atlantic without proper navigation aids, and I promise to describe a number of other similar incidents further on in the book.

CHAPTER NINE
"MOVING TO THE LEFT SEAT"

Captain Upgrade

The opportunity finally came for me in 1980 to get a shot at the left seat. We had a couple of captains who accepted positions with the major airlines. After all, non-sked flying is just temporary until one can move on to the better world of the majors. Of course, that is the main objective for everyone in the non-sked business.

I placed my name in the hat for the upgrade, which would be very unusual if I was accepted, as I was only a flight engineer. I think there were three guys who put in for upgrade. The insurance prerequisite for most of these companies required 1500 to 2000 hours of total flying time to qualify for the captain's position. I was one of two of the group who met the requirements. I was in good standing with the owner because of my mechanical experience and my ability to keep the airplane going in some cases. Naturally, I had to go to ground school all over again. Most of these schools were held in a motel somewhere, usually in a conference room. This one was not a big problem because we only had a few guys in the class.

The first part of schooling discussed the aircraft systems training. We then broke off into the flight training, which consisted of simulator and ground training and then the hands-on training in the airplane for preparation for the Federal Aviation Administration's (FAA) oral and flight check. The oral was not a big problem for me as it was basically the same test I had taken for the flight engineer certificate. With all that accomplished, we waited until there was an airplane and an FAA examiner available to do the check ride. We were doing the flight checks in Miami, so normally Dade Collier airport would be used, which is about twenty-five miles east of Miami.

I was the first one to get the check, scheduled to meet with the examiner who would give me the oral examination at Wag's Restaurant on 36th Street. When I walked into the "meeting place" and laid eyes on the examiner, to my surprise it was Clark Shadle, with whom I had just flown about a week earlier at the U.S. Air Force Reserve Unit at Charleston as flight engineer! Clark was an aircraft commander flying the C-141s. He remembered me very well, due to a little trick I once played on him at engine shut-down. I pulled all the shut-down circuit breakers. When he shut the engines down, he used the 1,2,3,4, sequence. I then pushed them back in, using the 4,3,2,1, sequence. He turned, not knowing what I had done, to look at me and asked, "What was that?" I said, "I don't know, sir," as though he and I *didn't* know. Considering the good-natured person he was, Clark actually enjoyed the prank, and we both had a big laugh together.

Back in the restaurant's "classroom," Clark's oral was strictly on the electrical system. He said if I could explain that system to him in detail, he would have no doubt that I knew the airplane. I had no problem because that was the area I studied the most. After all, I did rate first on the flight check, which arguably would make my position a little bit harder, because I would be the one who had to handle the engine-start problems, which sometimes are complicated.

We got it all done, and then we headed off to Dade Collier. The in-route operations went off normally, like keeping the airplane level, staying on course, and so on. The first is as a rule a normal approach, with a touch-and-go, and then you will probably lose an engine on the way around for a second landing. You will get almost to the point of touch down when another aircraft taxies onto the runway, so you have to go around with that engine shut down.

During these go-arounds, you are making different types of approaches in order to cover the entire requirement for the check. The examiner may or may not give you additional emergencies. It depends on how you are doing. After all the go-arounds, along with a few flight maneuvers, such as steep turns and stalls, you go back, you land the airplane, and you are finished. The next person then gets into the seat and does the whole thing over again. Clark also told my chief pilot that I gave him the best check ride he had seen on the Electra, and I danced inside my head with delight.

Once on the line, everything was virtually the same except that all of the responsibility rested on my shoulders now. If anything went wrong, the buck stopped with me. This was not a problem, as I was in the same position when flying as a flight instructor.

The non-sked business was a different type flying than normal airline operations. We did not have the luxuries the majors were used to, particularly the luxury of a single room at the motels. Sometimes we had to sleep all three crew members in the same room by ordering an extra cot for the additional person.

When we were at an outstation waiting for a trip, we had to provide our own place to stay. We would sometimes rent an apartment that we referred to as a "crash pad." There was normally always someone there, night or day. We had no maid service, so everyone had to clean their own mess. For the most part, the pilots would fly to the work place, and sometimes we would get together to purchase an old transport car, which we called the "airporter," which also had to be maintained by someone. When we had luck, we would have a good mechanic on the crew, normally the flight engineer.

To be a non-sked captain, it really helped to possess mechanical abilities on the aircraft you were flying, due to the fact that there would be many incidents that you would have to improvise in some mechanical problems to be able to make the flights. Some of the flight engineers were professionals in that field, but there also were the ones who were only flying as flight engineers to get the chance to upgrade to pilot. I had all the ratings myself and qualified in all fields: A&P and all three flight-engineer tickets. As I have mentioned before, if you know the electrical system on the Electra, you were way ahead of the game.

Every day of flying in the non-sked business would reveal some kind of problem. All the equipment was always marginal or not working at all. The radar was probably the biggest problem we had with most of the aircraft. Most of the radar units on these old airplanes were the old Bendix units, which had a tendency to pick up what was directly in front of you and to leave you wondering what was behind that. You virtually had to rely on the ATC to vector you around anything that was there, but sometimes that didn't work too well either. If, for example, the weather was really bad, the air-traffic controllers would turn the sensitivity down low so as to be able to see the aircraft but not the really bad stuff.

On a trip from Chicago one night, we were somewhere in the vicinity of Nashville, Tennessee. We ran into some unfavorable weather conditions, which had already ignited the St. Elmo's fire on the windshield and the propeller tips, calling to mind a Fourth of July fireworks. Actually, the windshield lit up like a Christmas tree, with little lines going everywhere. The discharge from the propeller tips looked very pretty bluish green in color.

The radar did not really paint the weather to be really bad, which would show real bright in the bad areas. When we started getting into some heavy turbulence, I asked the controller what it looked like to him. He said there was a solid area all the way past Nashville. I told him that we were in some real heavy turbulence, requesting a block altitude, usually a piece of space of about 4000 feet. The traffic controller okayed my request, declaring, in fact, that I could have any altitude I wanted, because there was no one in the area.

When he said that, I *knew* we were in some bad stuff, because the reason there was no one else there was because all other aircraft in the area probably had good radar units and were able to circumnavigate the bad stuff. Consequently, we had no alternative except to pound our way through the stuff. The Electra is not the smoothest airplane in turbulent conditions since fuel tanks are held rigidly in the stiff wings. When we finally reached the clearing on the other side, my copilot, as usual, sang his favorite Johnny Nash song, "I can see clearly now, the rain has gone."

I think the only way to survive this kind of flying is to hold onto a continued positive attitude and to try to contain the problems in a fun-type perspective instead of always getting in the panic mode. I think the secret to a lot of these problems, no matter how bad they get, is never to allow the other crew members seeing you sweat. When you can keep your cool and they notice it, most of them will adapt to the same mode. This has always been my theory and it worked most the time for me. As I mentioned before, there is virtually some kind of problem every day in the non-skedding business, so if you plan on continuing the employment, you must accept it as it is or seek an income elsewhere. I personally had no other choice at the time. I was destined to hang in there until something better came along.

We did have to fly by the rules under the FAR part 121 operational manual. We could only fly eight hours a day, thirty hours a week, or 100 hours a month, with a twelve-hour crew rest between the eight-hour days, if I remember correctly. That was in a single-crew condition. Occasionally, someone would try to take advantage of the ruling by fixing the log book or by flying over the restriction, which would get them into big trouble if they were caught, putting such individuals into a bind, because no fly, no money.

Everything was going very well for me. I was enjoying the flying, the crews with whom I flew, and the people for whom I worked. I tried to do everything in my power to get the cargo moved efficiently and punctually, which, in turn, encouraged the company owner to set us up for a dinner on him when we would do something special to make a trip go smoothly and on time. When the time came around for pay raises, my name, I'm pleased as tasty punch to say, always stood at the top of the list.

After a while, I was asked to be the check captain, requiring some more school and flight training. I didn't mind because the company would offset my pay during training. Besides, the check-captain's status would put added, relevant information on my resume just in case another better position came along, not to mention, of course, the additional revenue I'd earn doing the check rides. From then on, I usually had someone on every flight with me doing training of some sort. There were not very many Electra simulators around. So most the training was done in the aircraft. I think Eastern might have had an old simulator that most likely was not operational at that time. Anyway, it was much easier for us to use the airplane. In addition, flying as check captain gave me the opportunity to recommend some of the pilots with whom I had flown missions during my time with the Air Force Reserves. These guys were all officers ranked anywhere from "first looies" to colonels. I would fly as flight engineer for them in the military reserves and teach them to fly the Electra as civilian pilots. Some of them were flying as aircraft commanders with 1200 to 1500 total airtime hours.

I was then put on flying status for the USAF log-air contract that I was doing before as a flight engineer. We were based at Warner Robins AFB for this operation. The contract allowed us to take crew rests at the visiting officers quarters (VOQ), which were very nice, with maid service and all. We could also use the officers club for our dining and consume maybe a cocktail or so, of course, not within twenty-five hours of the next duty time. This was kind of like dying and going to heaven compared to how we lived doing the other flying.

The people we worked with were mostly civilians in civil service positions, the same as I was when working for the Air National Guard; as a result, we had a lot in common. On occasion, we would even go out to dinner with some of them. One of our crew members got to know one of the young ladies who worked there, so we had access to transportation anytime we wanted to go out somewhere other than to the officers club for dinner and a cocktail or two, or both, but not within twenty-five hours of our next scheduled flight, of course (some guys would swear the rule had more to do within twenty-five feet!). One of my favorite crew members was a young guy named Gil Ramsden, who occupied the flight-engineer seat until he got the opportunity to move up to the status of pilot with Southwest Airlines.

Gil named me "Lightning Rod," and there is a little story behind the name. We were flying a log-air flight between Langley, Virginia, and Seymour Johnson AFB. We already knew there were thunderstorms in the forecast. Once we got close to destination and the center turned us over to approach, we heard approach talking to a nearby KC-135 that had taken a lightning strike while flying through a thunderstorm area. Ground control was in desperate need to get the aircraft safely landed.

We could also see the weather on our radar screen, but the screen depicted a hole to go through to make a safe approach to the airport. Since ground control attempted to get the other aircraft on the ground first, the controller gave us a vector that would take us directly *into* the weather we were painting on the radar. We told the controller that, but he said that was the best he could at that time. We had no choice but to maintain that heading, and he would get us turned as soon as possible.

We continued on the heading and waited patiently for the instructions to make the turn. We were getting closer to the weather and started getting bounced around a little bit. Then the little bit became a big bit, then all of a sudden everything lit up when a big lightning bolt hit us, followed immediately by some very violent turbulence, along with a loud noise of something banging on the fuselage.

When we reported to the controller what we had experienced, he promptly gave us a vector to final approach to the airport. After the turn, the turbulence smoothed out a little, but it was still a bit rougher than we liked. We got down on final to about five miles out and into some smoother air when we broke into the clear and could see the runway. About the same time, however, we heard a loud "Whooom" noise accompanied by a bad vibration in the aircraft. We had come into contact with a small flock of birds, which got into the #4 engine to cause the vibration. I called for engine shutdown and continued the approach. Gil, the good engineer that he was, got the engine shut down and cleaned up very quickly and made it possible for me to continue on to land the airplane without any further ado. I taxied to the ramp and shut the airplane down. Not a very happy camper at this time, I went without delay to the control tower to voice a few nice, congenial words with the controller and requested to see the base commander.

The base commander realized that I was not a happy camper about this event and said he could definitely understand why. He apologized for all we went through and said he would do whatever we needed to take care of the problems we had. In due time, we discovered the source of the banging against the fuselage: these old airplanes have a high-frequency radio antenna (HF) that extends from right the top of the cockpit area all the way to the tail of the aircraft. The antenna snapped as a result of the lightning strike.

Air Force base maintenance brought out the "cherry picker," a long boom that would extend to the top of the airplane fuselage to disconnect the antenna to solve the banging problem. The next issue was to correct the bird damage, if any. The maintenance crew checked the engine and found no damage, with the exception of some bird parts that were still clinging to the propeller, requiring some elbow action along with some good cleaning solvent. After we all made a quick trip to the local men's room to clean our pants again, we returned to the airplane and took off for home to have our maintenance personnel have another look at the airplane to assure us there was no further damage to be found, while we headed for the bar to have a well needed jar or two—just another normal day of flying in the non-sked business.

CHAPTER TEN

"MAKE A LOT OF NOISE AND GO LIKE HELL! THE BEAUTIFUL BOEING 727!"

On to the Swept-Wing Jets

Fleming Airways finally started flying jets around 1982. Since I was high on the seniority list, I was one of the first to get a first shot at upgrading to these things. So here we go with the same old training scenario. First, the ground school for systems, and then the simulator, and finally to the airplane check ride. The best I can remember, there were three of us captains in the first class, together with copilots and flight engineers. All the training took place in Atlanta. We attended ground school at the Ho Jo (Howard Johnson Motel) located on Virginia Avenue by the airport. The best I remember, we used Delta simulators at their training center right at the airport.

Again, I had no problem with this part of the training. The airplane was just a tad different. This swept-wing, jet-powered thing was much different than flying straight-wing, propeller-driven airplanes. I had to get myself used to flying by the numbers (so to speak) rather than by the seat of the pants. Unlike the Electra, there was nothing instant about the jet. The instant response when the power was advanced was gone, the small rotation factor was different from the straight wing, and the climb angle was completely different. It was just a completely different flying machine.

I finally got to where I felt half-way comfortable with the thing, at least good enough to think I could get through the flight check. The flight check consisted of basically the same maneuvers and procedures as all the rest, but the difference in the airplanes was phenomenal. Anyway we "got-er" done and became jet captains.

We first got a contract flying for the Flying Tiger line operation as cargo carriers, flying mostly the same stuff we had been doing with the

Electras. We did manage to put our hands on some additional contracts with Flying Tigers, UPS, Emery World Wide, and the USAF log air. Some of the aircraft belonged to the company and some of the other companies just used our crews to fly their airplanes.

The maintenance was still the same on the aircraft our company owned—virtually non-existent. We *still* had to improvise a lot to keep them going, as the pay status was the same. We would still find a way to make the thing fly. On one occasion, I remember having a flap asymmetry problem. The flaps would get to a certain position and just stop, and the action took place in no particular position. I called maintenance about the problem, but there was no way a crew could get anyone to come out on the line to fix it. So rather than aborting the whole mission, which would also have cost us several days in repair, we put our heads together to see if we could figure a way to alleviate the problem. We parked the airplane, dug out the maintenance manual, and went to the bar to be able to have a jar to figure out this thing.

After some research in the manual, we found that the flap asymmetry was detected by the flap indicator on this particular airplane. So, if that were the case, we should be able to disconnect the indicator from the system and fly the plane. After a little rest, we decided to go back to the airplane to give it a try. After disconnecting the indicator, we had the flight engineer go outside to watch the flap position as we placed the handle in each position. The flaps appeared to be working perfectly, with the exception of no indication of their position. I felt comfortable with operating the aircraft that way and asked the other crew members what they thought. We all agreed to press on. Otherwise, we would be out of work for a few days without pay. I called the chief pilot and explained the situation to him. He gave us the go-ahead. We flew the thing for the rest of our schedule without any problems and returned the aircraft to the maintenance station when we finished.

We were still operating in the freight-dog business. So no matter what kind of aircraft we were flying, we still had the same problems of keeping the aircraft going so we could make money. That was the name of the game. I finally started flying the Emery contract, which was a lot better. At least we had some better maintenance on their planes. But it was still the freight-dog business. Everything went through the main hub located at Dayton, Ohio. This was a sort-by-day and haul-by-night operation. All the flights would start at the out station about dark thirty (a term used by cargo people meaning time to go to work) and end up in Dayton about 10 or 11ish at night. There were a few small lounge areas that were available on a first come, first served basis. It was virtually impossible to get any rest there though due to heavy snoring, flatulence, and things like that. The gourmet dining was done out of the nickel grabbers located in the company lunch room. Most of the pilots would gather there instead of trying to sleep. This place was full of flying war stories.

Most of this flying was virtually incident free. I do remember one trip though. We were coming out of Dayton one night on the way to Atlanta. My flight engineer was a long-standing friend of mine named Bill Looney, a true friend and one of the best flight engineers I ever flew with. We had just departed from Dayton and were on our initial climb. During this time, the flight engineer is very busy getting everything transitioned from on-the-ground status to in-the-air climbing mode, while also completing the checklist.

When he started the pressurization system, he noted that we were not pressurizing. When you are departing Dayton, it's kind of like turning a bunch of race horses loose at the starting gate. If one horse falls, it affects all the others behind him. So the best thing we could do was try to get the thing to pressurize to alleviate any problems of slowing the departure process. Bill told me to keep climbing to give him a chance to correct the problem. I did as he asked. I had lots of confidence in his ability. We went on oxygen as a safety precaution. I think we had reached about 15, 000 feet when Bill said he had found the problem, and we were finally pressurizing, which gave us all a relief. Bill had been with me a long time. He stayed with me about everywhere I went.

Air Atlanta
"LIKE DYING AND GOING TO HEAVEN"

The Beautiful Boeing 727-100– "If it ain't Boeing, I ain't going"

While still flying with the non-skeds, I had a layover in Atlanta sometime in 1985 for some reason and ran into a couple of old friends of mine, Gil Ramsden and Lloyd Puckett, with whom I had flown previously in the non-sked business. They were now with a new start-up, scheduled airline called Air Atlanta. After listening to their presentation about the airline, I decided, "What the heck! I might as well try to get involved in it."

After the interview, I found out firsthand about the remarkable qualities of the airline, an executive set-up with all first-class seating. The normal 727-100 had about 120 seats, where this one had only eighty-eight, lounge-style, leather-covered seats. The flight attendants all resembled movie stars, serving the passengers fantastic meals, together with real plates and silverware, most likely making passengers feel as though they had peacefully passed away and had gone to heaven. So I decided to make the change, providing I was accepted. I would actually have to take a dramatic cut in pay as a trade-off, but, on the other hand, I would be flying with a scheduled airline. I was hired as a captain, but would have to fly as copilot for a while before moving to the captain's seat, which didn't take very long considering how fast the airline expanded at the time.

Most of the flight crews were made up of ex-Eastern, ex-Continental, other airlines that had gone out of business for some reason or the other, and those who were tired of the freight-dog business. There were also three lady pilots. One of them I remember very well. Her name was Marylee Bickford. The first time I had her on a flight to JFK as my copilot, I climbed into my seat and looked over at her and said, "Heaven must be missing an angel." She asked, "Why is that?" I answered, "Because there's one sitting in your seat." She responded with that pretty little smile of hers and thanked me. In addition to her angelic qualities, she was very pretty and well endowed in the chest department.

After our arrival at JFK, we hit the taxi stretch along one of the airport's rough taxiways. I could not resist a glance at my copilot's bouncing chest. She simply looked back at me with that beautiful smile of hers. Nowadays, one would get called out for sexual harassment for that, but she was a very good sport as well as probably the best lady pilot with whom I have ever flown.

To complement the preceding paragraph, here's an incident, a favorable incident, in fact, that took place not on an aircraft but rather on a crew bus already bursting with crewmembers. One of our beautiful, young flight attendants was the last to board the bus and found no *full* seat available. She looked around then squeezed herself down next to the old Captain Mullins, a teasing action to get us old guys aroused, which wasn't a big problem. Some of these beauties were younger than my daughters.

After the bus arrived at our destination, she wiggled herself up and grabbed me by the arm to pull me to my feet as well. I had to admit to myself then that, while I'd be able to deal with life-threatening scenarios, I could not handle the embarrassing, erect situation *confronting* me at that moment. All the other flight attendants laughed until tears came to their eyes, and I exclaimed, "Hey, you guys! I may be old, but I'm not dead yet!"

Most of the ladies back then were in their early twenties, looked like models or movie stars, and were real party animals. All "BS" to the side, I remember *every* trip we took to Miami, beginning as an early morning flight and returning around two in the afternoon. These little cuties would always ask me if we were going to visit Woody's Lounge after the flight. A real airline environment, Woody's boasted old airline seats used as booths around the walls and sawdust on the floor, a place where many flight crews would gather after a long day in the air. In a slightly perverted way, Woody's resembled the kind of place my daughters, big smiles beaming across their cute little faces, would request for an ice cream cone, a request I could not resist. This old aviator was more than ready to go home once the clock had passed midnight, especially following an evening of watching the ladies performing breath-taking dances on table tops.

I had no place to stay, with exception of the expensive motels in the area, which would take a toll on the pocket book soon. One of the lady copilots, Clela Kranig, had a nice little place located on a little lake with a swimming pool and all just a few minutes from the airport. It was very fortunate for me to be invited to stay at her place along with some other pilots. The price was good and the living quarters were excellent.

Air Atlanta served basically as a feeder airline for Pan Am and had flights to JFK and to several airports in Florida, later adding charter flights for celebrities, due to the inviting 1st class cabin set-up. We carried people such as Bruce Springsteen's group, Chuck Norris, Marie Osmond, Tim Conway, and other notable people. The service was also inviting to the FAA, the "We are here to help you guys." It was not unusual to have at least one a day on someone's leg. Needless to say, the airline became noted as the perfect-party airline due to the complimentary alcohol drinks, the free food with all the trimmings, and the beautiful flight attendants. On some occasions, the flight attendants would provide free libations for the flight crew on layovers. Of course, everyone would abide by FAA's requirement (eight hours between "bottle to throttle"). Occasionally, a flight attendant would show up a little late for the return flight the next morning as a result of excessive party time.

We had lots of different personalities in this group of pilots, some very serious, some so-called comedians, and some who just didn't give a rat's ass. I enjoyed flying with this young copilot named Steve Zettler. Everything was a no-problem with Steve. No matter what situation you were in, he would always try to make it a comical one. He always said he thought I was the luckiest captain with whom he had ever flown. Whenever we experienced problem, I would always be able to come out of it smelling like a rose.

During one particular event, we were on a return flight from New Orleans. On landing, I had a left, main-gear tire blow. The aircraft veered uncontrollably to the left, with the help of a good cross wind, and it just so happened that a high-speed turn-off was right in my path. The first thing I heard was Steve laughing and exclaiming, "See! I told you so!" What else could I have said other than having experienced yet another lucky day? With no other alternative, I stopped the airplane on the high-speed and called for a tow.

It was virtually unheard of to have any major problems with maintenance on this airline. Air Atlanta's 727s were so well maintained and clean that you could eat your lunch on the landing gear door.

Speaking of the high-speed-turn-off incident reminds me of another crewmember named Harry "high-speed" Brown. Harry was a jewel of a guy. He was one of two black pilots with the company, that is to say, as best I can remember. Harry flew as copilot with me at Air Atlanta, and I ended up flying copilot for him at another airline that will be discussed in another chapter. Harry was one of the coolest people I have ever met. He told me about his experiences flying helicopters in Vietnam. I think I remember him saying he was shot down or had to ditch in the ocean nine times. He said after a couple of downings he started carrying his fishing kit in his flight gear so he could just go fishing the next time it happened.

A peach of a guy, Harry, following ATC directions, once vectored into a heavy thunderstorm area that almost removed the radar antenna from the nose of the airplane with hail. Needless to say, when I flew with Harry at another airline later on, I found out that there was no way that he would go anywhere near another thunderstorm if there was any way of avoiding it. I kept in touch with him for years after Air Atlanta.

We had old guys with thousands of hours of flight time and young fellows just starting into the business. The older guys were for the greater part excellent pilots, not the sort of new, prima-donna check-outs who represented the "ass holes" that you sometimes meet.

"One of those flight-attendants-urinating-in-his-coffee type," according to a senior flight attendant I called Trixie, who will appear in another chapter of this writing.

Virtually everyone was good people to fly with at Air Atlanta. Another guy I enjoyed flying with was Bob Bookhammer. I functioned with him as copilot a few times. Bob was one of those much laid-back types, who had spent time with Continental. His wife's maiden name was Mullins, the same as mine.

We once had a trip to pick up Bruce Springsteen and crew at Newark to carry them to Miami for a concert and then on to Dallas for another. Springsteen's group had leased the airplane and crew for the week for these outings. The Boss (as they called him) appeared to be a very nice person. It appeared that all his band members had lots of respect for him. As I understood, he was a very clean-cut guy, who allowed no pot smoking or things like that in his band. Captain Bob invited him up to the cockpit for awhile, which Springsteen enjoyed until we entered a little rain shower activity, including some lightning with some St. Elmo's fire on the windshield, all of which kind of got his attention. After we explained what it was and what caused it, he was okay. He was a very pleasant guy to talk to, just an everyday type of person. We dropped the musicians off in Miami and then headed back to Atlanta to arrive in the wee hours of the morning. Another crew was to go pick them up to take them to Dallas after the Miami showing.

Another celebrity who used us one time was Chuck Norris and crew at a time when Norris's film *Delta Force* premiered in Atlanta. We had the pleasure of carrying him and his crew to Atlanta for the grand opening. I was also flying copilot with Ron Arnold, or "Sky God," as the Air Atlanta people called him. Ron was a big guy, around 6' 2" tall and weighed about 220 or 230 pounds. He looked like someone you would see in the movies with his strong build. Needless to say, he and Chuck hit it off really well. Ron spent most of the flight in the rear with Chuck talking about body building and martial arts experiences and things like that, I would guess. We also allowed some of Norris's entourage to come up to view the cockpit, which was impressive to them.

I also had the pleasure of flying with the guy who kind of talked me into writing this book about my bush-pilot adventures, Al Morris. Al went through about the same thing I did. We both served in the Air Force. He piloted F-4s and I worked as a flight engineer. After our retirements, Al sent me a copy of his own book, *The Rogue Aviator,* a narrative that inspired me to write my own book about my own aviation experiences. When I had the first opportunity to fly together with Al, there was no doubt that this guy had eagerly engaged himself in aviation long enough to handle the airplane. I can always tell right off if you are looking at an old pro or at a newcomer by the way he holds the yoke. There's an old aviator's saying that goes something like this: "The old one holds it with his finger tips while the new one grips with both hands." We finger-tip flyers both became 727 captains at Air Atlanta.

This beautiful airline finally went into Chapter 11 and closed the doors in March of 1987. Evidently, the owners took the money and ran because to this day they still owe me $7,000, which I have erased any possibility of recouping. It actually appeared that the reason for starting the airline would result in financial benefit upon shut-down.

Independent Air/The Atlanta Skylarks Travel Club

"My Dream Comes True"—The Beautiful Boeing 707

I had already had the invitation in 1987 to fly with a company called Independent Air, which also incorporated a flying club known as the Atlanta Skylarks. The company also made use of the airplane of my dreams, the B-707, which as a kid I said I was going to fly some day. So now I had the chance to make my boyhood dreams come true.

Not only did Independent Air work as a flying club, the company also served as a charter carrier, chartering mostly down into the Caribbean, to Mexico, with some international trips to Europe including Germany, Spain, and Italy as well as gambling junkets to Biloxi, Mississippi, Atlantic City and Las Vegas. To name a number of flight destinations, we hit St. Pitts, Guadeloupe, Martinique, St. Lucia, Barbados, and Santa Domingo in the Dominican Republic. In Mexico, we landed at Zihautanejo, Puerto Vallarta, Ixtapa, Cancun, and Cozumel in the Yucatan Penal. Other destinations included Porto Prince in Haiti, Georgetown in Guyana, San José in Costa Rica, Caracas in Venezuela, and Bogotá in Columbia.

I already had a reliable connection with Independent Air through Don Jackson, a friend of mine from our days together in the Tennessee ANG doing the tanker refueling. He also worked for the FAA as an air traffic controller at the AARTC center in Hampton, Georgia. Don had previously asked me if I had an interest in flying on a part-time basis with Independent, an offer I had to turn down because of a potential conflict with my flying status at the time with Air Atlanta.

I mentioned to another one of my friends at Air Atlanta, a gentleman named Kenny Carroll, that I intended to transfer to Independent Air. On my recommendation, Kenny decided to go along with me. We completed ground school together at a company office located along the Atlanta airport loop road. The main office for the company was located at Smyrna, Tennessee, where the old Stewart AFB once thrived.

Along with some flight engineers, Kenny and I were the only two pilots in the class. Our instructor was Chief Engineer Ray Allan, who, like me, once lived in the same area in Tennessee. Since the B-707 and the B-727, which I had already been flying, were both Boeing equipment, the systems were very much the same; consequently, I had no problem at all with the conversion.

After the ground school, we were ready to hit the simulator. We used American Airlines' training facility in Dallas, Texas, which was the only one remaining with B-707 simulators. The closer I got, the faster my old heart would pound. I was actually going to get to fly the airplane I had always dreamed of flying! The cockpit is virtually the same as the 727 except for the four throttles instead of three and some other features of minimum difference.

I normally don't get excited about much, but I was really excited about this transition to the B-707, which I had wanted to fly since I was just a kid. As usual, I crawled my butt into the driver's seat and tried to act like it was old school again, as I have always done. Everything resembled the cockpit of the 727. However, when we started to fly this thing, I found out right away that this big monster was like getting out of a toy car into a Cadillac. It was so much more stable than the 727. You could virtually line this big thing up on final approach and just turn it loose, providing you had no cross wind or anything. On the other hand, unlike the 727, a more advanced machine, when you turned the 707, you would turn the control and wait a couple of seconds. Then the airplane would start moving. Once I got these idiosyncrasies down, I was ready to go.

The training syllabus was virtually the same as all the other transitions, so I would not go into that again on this airplane. Most of our training was done at night, due to others using the same simulator or maintenance being done during the daytime hours. I would take several simulator periods to complete the training. We had two captains performing two hours each every night. Once we both jumped through all the hoops well enough to satisfy the check captain, we did the same thing over again by taking an oral with the FAA examiner and then the simulator check with the same examiner.

I was picked as the first one to go. The person who gave us the simulator training rode the right seat for the check ride. Everything went very well through the entire ride until we got to the point where I had to perform the missed approach with one engine shut down. Then the problem started. During the simulator training, we trained with the #1 engine shut down for this maneuver, but this time the FAA examiner had us shut down the #4 engine instead. When we reached the go-around position, and I needed to use the rudder to keep the airplane straight, I was so programmed to the other rudder that I pushed the wrong rudder and got myself into an uncontrollable condition, from which I couldn't recover. As a result, I didn't pass the check ride, a big surprise to everyone, especially to me.

The examiner requested an additional four hours of simulator training then to have me to return for another check. The company put a second check captain to work, a fellow named Mark McDonald, to take me through the training and the check ride with the FAA. I passed the next one with flying colors. I was then a happy camper. Later on, I myself became chief pilot and check captain for the company. You can bet your sweet bippy that, from that day forward, I would always rotate the engine to be shut down for go-around training. It was a lesson well learned. I chalked it up as a good lesson, and I may well have saved somebody's life.

My first initial operating experience flight (IOE) turned into an interesting experience. Captain Mark McDonald was my check captain. The flight went from Boston to Punta Delgada, Azores—just a normal passenger trip that the company had a contract to fly. Everything was going as scheduled, with no expectations of any problems. The weather was good for a very smooth flight. When the Oceanic controller turned us over to Santa Maria approach and gave us all the information on the approach, Mark got into the flight bag to pull out the approach plates for the approach. No approach plates could be found. The last crew had misplaced them, or someone had taken them out for revision purposes. At any rate, here we were, ready to start our descent for the approach with no directions on how to do it. The sky just happened to be overcast at the airport, so we couldn't make a visual approach. Mark was on the radio with approach control in an attempt to get some information on the approach procedure, but he had no luck. At the same time, there was another aircraft on the ground getting ready for departure. The pilot overheard our conversation with the tower, immediately offering to read the directions from his own plate. Naturally, Mark went for it and wrote the information down.

Mark then advised approach that we were ready for the approach, so we were cleared. The approach was a VOR (VHF Omni-directional range), which meant we had to descend to 3000 feet, to cross the VOR, and to fly outbound on a heading to make a left turn to intercept the runway heading inbound. I suggested to Mark that I thought we should stay at 3000 feet until we crossed the VOR before we started our descent on final approach to prevent the possibility of contacting a mountain top or something. Of course, he did not disagree. We passed the VOR and started our normal descent rate of about a three-degree slope. When we finally broke out of the clouds and had the runway in sight, we knew that we were too high for a normal approach. We could either use more flaps to get down or do a visual go-around and land.

I suggested forty degrees of flaps to get down and to take a look at the situation. If it looked safe, we could continue to land; if not, we could still go around. I knew that once we got the airplane into the slot for a safe landing, we would require a lot of power to get us on the ground. With the flaps at forty degrees (which is full down), they are like barn doors hanging out there in a mighty wind. We were lined up beautifully. I saw no reason to go around, and we continued on toward the runway. Mark still reminded me of the need for lots of engine power. The landing ended up being a greaser (a very smooth landing), according to the captain who had provided us with the approach information. Certainly out of safety and respect, he waited and watched. We thanked him for his support and wished him and his crew and passengers a pleasant, safe trip to their destination. Just another mission accomplished.

I finally got all my checks completed and started flying revenue trips. I think the first flying I did was out of Boston to the Azores, the same airport that we were at earlier on my IOE training. As I understood the situation, the people we delivered lived at the Azores and worked for a company in Boston. I don't really know the details on how all this was handled. I just know that we flew them from Boston to the Azores and picked up another group of people for the return to Boston. The runway at Punta Delgada was too short for takeoff with a full load of passengers and fuel. However, because there was always enough residual fuel aboard from the inbound flight, we took off and flew to Santa Maria, which lay just about twenty minutes away to refuel for the return trip.

These coastal airports are all about the same. Normally, the initial approach altitude for all of them is 3,000 feet. There is some pretty high terrain a short distance inland in this particular area, and I plan to provide more detail later on.

We did experience a particularly large problem with carrying these people: the weight that was going onto the aircraft. I noticed that the aircraft always felt heavier than what the weight and balance said it was, so I started doing some observation on the loading. The normal baggage weight we used for the weight-and-balance figuring came to about seventy-five pounds. I watched the service personnel lifting and carrying these pieces of luggage, noticing they really struggled to move them to the airplane from the cart. Out of great curiosity, I wanted to check this out for myself, so I headed down to look it over.

The first bag I tried to pick up was so heavy that I could barely get it off the ground. I asked one of the bag smashers to open it up for me. This bag was completely full of canned food, which probably weighed close to 200 pounds! If every passenger's bag weighed that much, the airplane had to be way over weight.

I also noticed very questionable things going into the cargo hold: car bumpers, fenders, and other car parts. It appeared that there might be a little payola going on around the old cargo-handling department. Evidently, the things they intended to carry out of there were not available to buy in the Azores; consequently, they overloaded our airplane to get it there.

After some additional probing, I found out that the bags were not being weighed at all! Then, too, no one would admit knowing *anything* about the other things that were being loaded onto the airplane. I mentioned this to the loading supervisor, letting him know that I was going to have to check it on each flight in the future. After that I noticed a big change in how the aircraft felt on the takeoff roll. I remembered reading about a DC-8 crash not too long before that on takeoff from one of those airports up there. The aircraft was found to have been overweight by about 10,000 pounds! These are the things that most likely would not happen with a scheduled airline. A real good friend of mine named Rich Hazen lost his life because of something similar while flying a Value Jet flight out of Miami. I flew with Rich at a couple of airlines before he went to Value Jet. He was one of the nicest people I ever met.

I remember very well one particular trip to the Azores. We were at the Azores Santa Maria airport to refuel and to pick up our return flight plan to Boston. The ground crew had finished fueling the plane but hadn't brought out our flight plan yet. I called them on the radio and questioned them about it. They advised me that the flight hadn't arrived yet. They said that their computer had been down all morning, the flight plan hadn't come up yet, and they didn't know for sure when it would. Naturally, we had a load of passengers on board, and they grew very restless after we waited for awhile on the flight plan. After about an hour of waiting with passengers becoming more restless, we decided we had to do something. We still had the flight plan we used to get there, so we decided we would just fly back on the same plan. We called Oceanic—the only control that pilots have when flying over the ocean. Oceanic has no radar, and all the reporting points are North-South, East-West coordinates, which depict geographical reporting points that are entered into the navigations system to fly by (a very antiquated navigations system, you might say)—after we got airborne and received an okay. The route had not changed that much although we did receive a different altitude. Everything proceeded well until we got about an hour out, finding ourselves in some pretty rough turbulence. We hoped the turbulence would last only as a temporary disruption, so we put up with it for a while.

In a few minutes, the turbulence got so bad that I had to ask for a higher altitude. As we knew then, Oceanic was very slow at these kinds of things as they had no radar and had to rely on other aircraft-position reports to make determinations. Finally, Oceanic determined that FL 390 (39,000 feet) would be clear for us. We climbed to FL 390 where the turbulence was the worst I had ever seen during my flying career.

Everything was going everywhere! The flight attendants screamed at us from the rear. I looked out the side window at the wings, and our flying machine greatly resembled a paper airplane: the wings and the engines bouncing around violently. The turbulence got to the point where we just couldn't stand it anymore, so I call Oceanic and advised them that we had to descend. They told me to hold on for a few minutes while they checked on it. I told them that I could not wait a few minutes, and I initiated a descent to FL 370 wherc I was before (I didn't think there would be a problem with that altitude because we just came from there). On my way down to 370, I requested 350, which they did after checking for other aircraft separation.

After we got settled down at FL 370, we noticed that our ground speed decreased due to the increased head wind that we had encountered. I asked my flight engineer to re-calculate our fuel to assure we were going to be able to make it to Boston with this ground speed. After re-calculating, he advised that, if this head wind continued, we probably would not have enough fuel to make it to Boston. Naturally, I was very concerned and started to think of the option of landing someplace else if need be. The wind could get worse or it could improve, but we wouldn't know until we continued farther west. All we could do was keep on going and hoping. We definitely didn't want to tell the passengers anything and get them in an uproar. We flew on for about another hour but realized no change. The next thing to do was to start checking weather at other airports, which I turned over to the copilot. While we were doing this, the engineer looked at me with a big smile and exclaimed, "Guess what?" By his smile, I knew what he was going to say: the wind had dropped off some, and normally when that happens, it will continue dropping, which, to our good fortune, it did. We continued on to Boston with no further problems.

Only on rare occasions would we have those smooth days when nothing went wrong in this kind of business. Interestingly enough, we actually experienced not one single problem on our next trip to the Azores. The airplane checked out okay. Cargo loading went along fine. Our passengers seemed content and delighted, all in all an unbelievable day, yet one of those days you know is not going to last. Everything went as smooth as silk on the trip over to the Azores. We all went to the motel for our crew rest, which we did on every trip. The motel, according to several people, was supposed to be haunted. Even a couple of our flight attendants reported that they had seen odd things happen there. A woman dressed in a white dress, kind of like a wedding dress, they said, made her way through the wall, walked around their rooms, returned to the wall, and disappeared. The attendants recounted the story to the desk clerk only to learn that the desk clerk had heard the same story time and time again.

Not believing in ghosts, I just kind of laughed and forgot about it. Later on, however, a couple of others said they had witnessed the same thing, so I will leave it to you to believe it or not. It's a good conversation piece anyway. The main thing that I liked about this motel was that you could check in, go to your room, and get naked or whatever you liked while waiting for the service people to bring you a nice breakfast of your choice. The facility also had a nice pool out back for those who liked to recline in the sun by the pool, and that's where the flight attendants would mostly spend their time—except when they slept, of course.

Our return trip was about the same as the inbound flight, with the exception of normal problems, such as overloading the airplane with an excess number of people, which was an ongoing thing. Have you ever seen an eighteen-year-old lap child? This would actually happen at times. They would try *anything* to get an extra body on the airplane.

Everything was just going too well on the return flight to Boston: very smooth with not a cloud in the sky. We had virtually no head wind on this day, really just one of those unbelievable days. We were getting within about an hour out when we normally would receive the airport weather report in order to avoid any surprises that would trigger a safe deviation. Boston weather had worsened since we departed earlier in the day, now offering very low clouds and poor visibility. At least we knew what to expect when we arrived, so we continued on.

After Oceanic turned us over to the ATC, we were able to get a better picture of the weather conditions. We found that Boston's weather had deteriorated, and the visibility was fluctuating at this time. We continued on toward Boston, hoping to experience weather conditions good enough to get in when we did get there.

The control center then turned us over to Boston approach control. As soon as we changed to approach, we could overhear radio transmissions about missed approaches, diversions, and all the bad stuff that we were not looking forward to. We still aimed to make the approach, to find the runway, and to land in order then to head for the bar to have another jar, but the scenario we had imagined was not going to be the case this time. After trying the approach and missing, we had no choice but to go to the open alternate, namely to Providence, Rhode

Island. We flew on to Providence and were able to get in, but we landed at about 12:30 a.m. on a Monday morning when there was not very much going on at that time. We did, however, have an even greater problem: there were no customs people at this airport to clear all our passengers arriving from the Azores!

We were still able to contact Boston approach control. We told them of the problem. Their reply was that all the customs people had left for the night because they had no international arrivals until about eight in the morning. They said they would try to round up a crew to send to us, and that we should keep all the people on board until further notice. This news made some passengers very unhappy when we passed the information on to them.

I had been exposed to this same kind of situation before and knew that it could lead to total chaos. I decided to direct the flight attendants to provide the passengers with comp drinks and whatever food we had left on the plane. Perhaps we could get their bellies full of food and their heads intoxicated with enough alcohol that they would go to sleep. This worked fine for the most part, with the exception of a few diehards who kept complaining to the extent of threatening to cut the seats up in the airplane and things like that. I guess some of them just got claustrophobia from confinement to the inside of the plane or something and became really violent.

After about a two-hour delay, we received a call from Boston that the weather had greatly improved, and, if we liked, we were welcome to try to come on to Boston. With a sigh of relief, I told Boston that we would *definitely* give it a try. I immediately got on the PA and passed on the news to the passengers, who understandably responded with lots of audible cheering and clapping. We got the old 707 cranked up again and proceeded on to Boston to end this trip out of hell. As they say, "Some days you are the bug, and some days you are the windshield." We definitely deserved a jar at the bar on this day.

This next little adventure trip was somewhat different from the previous ones. We were assigned a ferry trip to the Azores to pick up a load of passengers and to take them to Barbados. We fired up the old 707 and prepared ourselves for the next trip. On the trip, I had a new copilot, with whom I had not yet flown. At that time, we were using the

Omega navigation system, which was nothing compared to the sophisticated satellite systems in use today.

The flight engineer was my old faithful and favorite Bill Looney, who is also named in another story in the book. The four flight attendants with us were old favorites as well: Trixie, Pixie, Dixie, and Bob. Most of the flight attendants consisted of ex-Eastern, ex-Air Atlanta employees, including some from other airlines that went "tits up" (belly up or bankrupt) for some reason other. Some of the ladies flew just for the love of flying; some took to the air for the money; some put on their uniforms for the adventure of travel to distant points on the planet; and some joined the aviation world simply to get away from home life and boredom. We had all kinds.

Some were real party animals, too! I remember one occasion when we all had to stay for a while in Madrid, Spain. An inner spark— perhaps a psychic awareness—propelled me to the top of the motel, where the pool was located. When I arrived, I looked around and noticed that the ladies were all lying by the pool with nothing on but the little thing around their butt called a bikini bottom. They all thought they were disguised, sporting their little hats and wide-brimmed sunglasses. Looking a little closer, I recognized Trixie, Pixie, and Dixie. Poor Bob missed a sight for sore eyes. What could I do but just take my place in the sun and, like the ladies said, "When in Spain, do as the Spaniards do." Case closed.

Back to aviation, Trixie, Pixie, and Dixie also had their way to distract me. On one flight, we were flying along fat, dumb, and happy, enjoying ourselves with the ladies and happily consuming the food and drinks they brought to us. Flight Engineer Bill Looney—always the clown—was up to his usual antics.

Bill had a little red warning light at the top of the engineer's panel. He also kept a "hidden" switch that he could turn on and off—thus turning on and off the red light—without drawing attention to his actions. Trixie already had seen him do it before, but Pixie hadn't. When Pixie entered the cockpit, he would turn the light on; when she walked out, he turned it off. She finally noticed the thing and asked Bill for an explanation. Bill told her that the light determined the difference between the hot women and the cold women. He told her to step out the door to prove his point; she exited the cockpit, and the light went out; when she stepped back in, the light came on. I think she was kind of in between believing or not believing Bill's story. During the entire trip, Bill kept doing the same thing over and over until Trixie finally spilled the beans to Pixie.

Anyway, during all of these fun-and-game antics, the new copilot was playing with the navigation system. I really was not paying that much attention to what he was doing. I didn't think there was much he could tear up, but I was wrong. Somehow he had toyed enough with the navigation system that we went off course. I believed he had deleted some of the coordinates, resulting in a course shift. Normally, the route is pretty much in a virtually straight line, with maybe some very small turns, if any. At any rate, we lost our Omega navigation system. We were pretty close to half way across already, so my decision was to continue on. We had two ADF radios, which were both working well. I tuned in the Ascension Island beacon, and we were already on the Flores beacon located at the Azores. I pulled out the map and matched the bearing to the coordinates on the flight plan and pressed on toward the destination.

We asked Oceanic for flight level 410, making it safer for other traffic separation. We could go to this level because we were light, due to the fact that we carried no passengers at this time. When we matched the bearings from Ascension to the coordinates, we would give our position reports, which worked out just fine. This was another one of those improvising situations. After landing at Santa Maria, I definitely had to have a nice heart-to-heart talk with my young, playful copilot. That was the only trip I flew with that copilot. When I ran into him about five years later at a Miami motel, he said he was flying captain on a 747 for a cargo carrier.

After the Boston tour, I was relocated to Denver. Actually, my whole crew relocated there, to include Trixie, Pixie, and Dixie. We picked up Betty Boob instead of Bob this time. Of course, Bill remained with me. Bill and I always tried to stay together—except when he decided he would go try out Japan Air Lines (JAL) for awhile. I could only wish him well. After maybe six months with JAL, he called me to let me know that he would like to rejoin our group. By that time, I had achieved the position of chief pilot, so I had enough influence to get him back. Of course, he was non-current in the 707, so naturally he had to complete a short training program before he could fly. When he finished, he was right back flying with me again.

Out of Denver, we flew for the most part to Mexico, to Jamaica, and to other coastal vacation spots in the Virgin Islands. They were all vacation charters by contract from a company located in Denver (one of those companies that sometimes paid salaries on time and sometimes not at all). In any case, this was international flying, so we were able to make the trip down and back in one day. We also did some junkets to Las Vegas and Atlantic City on some occasions. You have to know that these were vacation trips, and, when people are on vacation, they just kind of let it all hang loose. It was not unusual for some of them to be almost intoxicated when they boarded the airplane. The dress code was nonexistent. You might even see some lady board with only a coat and nothing underneath, all but announcing, "Party time is here!"

We also made trips from Denver to Las Vegas. On one memorable morning flight to the city of twenty-four-hour entertainment—our feet up and enjoying a cup of joe at the top of the climb—Betty Boob, our newest flight attendant, rushed into the cockpit to inform me that a couple in the last seat to the rear of the airplane had covered themselves completely with a blanket. The blanket, she said, was undulating up and down. I assumed that such a sight would have been unusual for Betty. As though I was concerned, I continued to listen to her story. I asked her if they were disturbing anyone besides her. She gestured that no one else appeared disturbed. I then advised her not only *not* to alarm the blanketed passengers until they had completed their act, but also to let them know they shouldn't do it again. Got to keep everyone happy, you know. On that kind of flying, it got to a point that nothing much could be considered unusual any more.

We had another little incident one time coming out of Montego Bay. A young lady boarded with her boyfriend. She looked sick to me as she walked across the ramp to the airplane. He nearly had to carry her onto the airplane. The attendants and the boyfriend got her to the back of the airplane and put her in a seat. It was a very hot day there, and we had no air conditioning on this airplane until we got the engines running, which made matters worse.

Trixie appeared in the cockpit to talk to me about the situation, declaring that the woman was in a bad way, continually placing cold towels on her head, and tying up at least one of the flight attendants. I then asked Trixie to bring the boyfriend to me. After discussing the situation, I found that she had been in the hospital, and the doctors were unable to help her, and now he was trying to get her back to Denver.

After thinking about this for awhile, I realized that this was not the kind of problem that *we* should take on. More importantly, we were definitely *not* equipped medically to help this woman. She really needed an air-evacuation aircraft with at least a nurse on board. I then called for one of the boarding agents and explained my decision. They then called the ambulance to take her back to the hospital.

Not long after we arrived back in Denver, the company called me to verify my version of the event. Evidently, someone attempted to blame me for her death because she passed away not long after we departed. I detailed exactly what happened and how it happened. Company officials also got the same story from the flight attendants who performed at their best to make the woman comfortable. The company concluded that I had done the right thing. That was the last I heard of that incident.

As I have previously said, there was never a dull trip with this type of operation. We were at the same place a few trips later, getting ready to depart from Montego Bay in Jamaica. Everything was going fine for a change. The airplane was full as usual, our takeoff weight was right up to the max as usual, and the weather was very hot—as usual.

About an hour after departure, flight attendant Trixie came to the cockpit with consternation reading all over her face to inform me that an older lady had gone into the ladies restroom and had been there for an excessive amount of time. Trixie said she had already tapped on the door but got no answer. We had a way to open the door if need be, so I told her to get some help and to open the door to check things out. The elderly lady, we learned, had passed out.

Trixie and her helper managed to lift the unconscious woman out of the restroom and carried her to a place on the floor in the cabin. With the assistance of the first-aid kit, they attempted to revive her. Trixie feared the woman had died. I immediately vacated my seat to look more closely at the situation, noticing, to the good fortune of the ailing woman, that she was still breathing—but very slowly. Her stomach contracted and expanded enough to indicate she still had life in her.

I then asked for a doctor via the PA system. Most doctors, in my experience, are hesitant to take actions in cases like this one. Nobody responded to my call for assistance; however, a young lady then came forward to declare she was in medical-school training and wanted to offer help. I had no choice really so I accepted.

After the would-be doc checked her unconscious patient, she advised me that she needed immediate help. She said we should land as soon as possible at the nearest airport where the woman could receive professional medical attention. At the time, we were only about a half hour from Cancun, so I advised the passengers that we were going to have to head for Cancun for a medical emergency.

The passengers must have accepted the decision without second thought, considering the possibility that any one of them may have experienced a similar situation. My copilot notified the company, and the company then advised Cancun handlers to prepare themselves to receive the ill woman and to take care of our turn-around with fueling, flight plan, and any other necessary items to continue our original trip.

However, we figured we had not yet burned off enough fuel to bring the airplane down to a safe landing. I had two choices: to dump some real expensive fuel or try to land this thing way overweight, an action which would require a very smooth, grease-job landing, which can be very hard to do under this kind of stress.

I decided to go for the latter. Thank God that it happened to be a real calm day, with no cross wind to speak of! The landing was so smooth that I couldn't believe it myself—one of those hand-clapping-in-the-cabin landings. We hadn't declared an emergency or anything, so when we got on the ground, the ground-control person evidently did not know of our on-board problem. He stopped us in place to let another airplane in front of us, which really got me disturbed. I cautioned him that we needed to get to the parking area immediately.

He said he didn't realize we had any problem. I responded that *he should have noticed the ambulance waiting for us at our assigned gate.*

Anyway, we got the lady there to be taken care of and went on our way back to Denver. When we got back, the director of operations (DO) called me again to compliment me that I was making quite a name for myself with sick-and-dying people during the recent past. I figured he really meant the preservation of big money for not dumping fuel, a major expense. So off to the bar we went for another jar or two—again, never a dull day in the non-sked business.

I think it was about this time that I received promotion to chief pilot and check captain of the operation. But I accepted on the grounds that my office would have me working out of the Atlanta office instead of Smyrna, Tennessee. The company okayed the condition. I would travel to Smyrna about once a month for a few days to get all the flight records straightened out for the FAA to view whenever these fellows happened to come around. Occasionally, I would have to go to the simulator in Dallas for training. I would also perform the flight checks on the normal trips.

We continued to fly these same routes, experiencing the same old problems discussed earlier. After a few months, we acquired a contract that placed us at Montego Bay as our home base, while flying the same type flights, except that we operated there on flights to Spain and California. In Denver and Chicago, we had to deal with temperatures soaring below 0 degrees Fahrenheit, including lots of snowy and icy conditions.

In Montego Bay, on the other hand, we housed ourselves comfortably in a nice motel located atop a hill overlooking the entire area, including the bay, which was like dying and going to heaven compared to the other places. The motel encircled a large swimming pool, with palm trees and lots of tropical growth swaying back and forth in the warm wind, resembling a tropical travel brochure. Of course, all the flight attendants liked to spend time by the pool to keep their young, hard bodies nice and tan. The guys, of course, sat there as well, a cold beer in one hand and one eye on the ladies.

I *really* remember one incident in the wee hours of the morning, probably around two. We were all in the pool taking lessons in water survival since we were now flying mostly over water. On this particular occasion, we had reached the being-naked-in-the-water phase of the training, ending up with an emphasis on how to get your pants on rapidly when the desk clerk received a complaint of noise and disturbance at the pool. Have you ever tried to slip back into your swimming trunks while fully immersed in water after the motel clerk turned the pool lights on in an attempt to determine the basis for the complaint? You should try it sometime. As you can see with this example, we were not *always* in an in-flight-emergency situation while on the job.

My crew and I had the understanding from briefing to briefing that whatever went on anywhere *during* flights would remain *with* the flights. It's virtually impossible for crews to spend so much time together away from home without falling into some sort of extracurricular activity at one point or another. After all, we are human beings. As captain, of course, I did not participate in such activities. Tsk, tsk, tsk, tsk. Boys will be boys and girls will be girls. For most of our flights, though, we'd have Trixie, Pixie, or Dixie along with us. Since many of our passengers did not drink, all three of them would make sure the crews had later access to "left-over" comp drinks not consumed on the flights.

These amounted personally to the best flying conditions I had encountered up to this point. We were normally on a two-weeks-on-and-one-week-off schedule in order to stay in line with flight-time restrictions. Furthermore, we were allowed 120 hours each month for international flying, which was a much better way to build time as compared to domestic flights. After all, the name of the game was mostly money, excluding the retired military people who just wanted to fly airplanes. We had married flight attendants, who were only in it to be away from the boredom at home or perhaps for reasons not necessarily related to making money or serving people in the cabin.

As for myself, I was lucky enough to get all of the flying that I wanted. I was also making extra dough via my position as check captain. I spent a lot of time conducting simulator training and ground school for new pilots or pilots due for the required check rides, normally once a year for copilots and every six months for captains.

We would also have layovers in areas of Europe, including all the islands noted earlier, along with a few locations in the U.S. Some of the younger crew members who had never been in other countries really enjoyed this kind of aviation experience. Some of them had never been out of their home state. It was something really new to them and a great adventure for these young pilots.

As the captain, I always had trip money that was a standard part of the flights to carry in case of unexpected scenarios. Sometimes the young flight attendants would over spend their allowance by partying too much and would have to hit me up for a loan, and I would try to provide to help them out. It wasn't unusual to return to home station with a pocket full of IOUs to turn in with my expense account. If the borrowers didn't pay it back, payroll would take it out of their next pay check.

We also flew some charter trips to Germany, permitting us to stay there with the passengers for a week. We rotated crews on a weekly basis. The inbound crew would stay, and the crew that had been there for a week would work the return trip with the passengers who were there. I had an opportunity to take my wife, Pat, along with me on one of those trips. I had been in Germany many times during my Air Force and Air National Guard days and knew the lay of the land quite well.

After Pat and I checked into the hotel located just outside the airport, we gathered up enough things to spend a few days traveling and hit the *Autobahn* (freeway). I decided to take Pat up the Rhein River as far as Remagan, a city whose bridge—although already heavily damaged by the German *Wehrmacht* (Army) during World War II to slow down the progression of American troops—served as a psychological advantage to the advancing Americans in pursuit of the retreating *Wehrmacht* forces, improving Allied morale and communicating disaster to the German army. According to General Dwight D. Eisenhower, who would later become the 34th U.S. President, "The bridge is worth its weight in gold." The bridge, known as the Ludendorff Bridge, eventually collapsed fully into the Rhein River.

I had visited Remagan many times before. My flight crews started going there back in the mid 60s when we were doing the Creek Party refueling operation for the Air Force. One of our fellow guardsmen had a brother who died at the bridge during the war, and he wanted to see the place that cost his brother his life.

We all got to know the *Bürgermeister*, or mayor, there in Remagan. He and his family grew very receptive to us, and thus began a lasting friendship between them and the Tennessee people. Whenever Pat accompanied me on flights to Germany, we normally ended up spending time at the mayor's family hotel. In fact, the *Bürgermeister* and his family also visited us all in Knoxville, Tennessee.

Aside from our visits with the mayor and his family, my wife and I continued to check in at the same hotel. All in all, Pat could only praise the German hospitality that embraced us. After the morning's *Frühstück und Kaffee* (breakfast and coffee), we headed for the historical sites, itching to see more and more over the next few days. We would tour all day long and usually stay for the night at one of the nearby *Gasthaüser* (guest houses).

Pat's gone for the Knight

Germany's castles—such magnificent stone fortresses—were built in medieval times to help protect against invasion and to guard newly acquired wealth. For some unfortunate individuals, they also served as places of torture as evidenced by the torture chambers, some of them still pretty much intact, their punishment equipment still hanging on the walls and other pain-causing items displayed on the floors. Fascinating to my wife, the castles typically sat at the top of a hill, offering a spectacular view of the river and surrounding countryside. We even stayed at one of the castles that had been made into a hotel perched on top of a hill overlooking the Rhein River. We must have passed numerous rolls of Kodak film through our camera!

Pat at the hotel with the Rhein River below

The company also had a B-727 on which I was able to maintain my currency by taking required training just in case I was needed to fly this sweetheart. Life treated us pretty well back then.

Gulf Air
(Trans Ocean Airways)

This is one long airplane—The DC-8-61

After a few years, around early 1989, I learned that Gulf Air needed pilots. I received a call from an old friend and ex-chief pilot at Air Atlanta, Jim Reddy, now with Gulf Air as chief pilot. The company, he informed me, had acquired DC-8 aircraft and needed pilots. He made it perfectly clear that he could hire me in a captain's position, but I would probably have to fly a short period as copilot before the transition could take place. Although I wasn't all that interested in leaving Independent Air, I did want to pursue a type rating in the DC-8. To accomplish this would open up several more job opportunities because lots of freight carriers were using DC-8s at this time.

The training with Gulf Air would take place at the company office in Essex, Pennsylvania, a small suburb just west of the Philadelphia airport. I checked in at the motel, threw my bags onto the bed, and proceeded to the bar. When I entered the bar, I encountered a great surprise. There sat Harry "High-Speed" Brown, a friend of mine from Air Atlanta, undergoing DC-8 training with Gulf Air. I hadn't seen Harry since Air Atlanta, and we had a lot of catching up to do. Harry said he had been hanging around home playing with his *real* race car (explaining why we named him "High-Speed" Harry) and arguing with "the old lady" and was more than ready to get back into flying. I think

Jim Reddy had contacted some of the other guys from Air Atlanta as well, but they hadn't showed yet.

We had been in Gulf Air's ground school for a couple of weeks when I got a call from another friend of mine advising me that one of the crews I had been flying with at Independent Air had crashed one of the 707s with a load of Italian passengers in route from Bergamo, Italy, to Montego Bay, with a fuel stop at the Azores. The 707 crashed into the top of a mountain on approach into Santa Maria, Azores, killing everyone on board. It took me a while before I could gather my thoughts to do anything, knowing these people were the same people I had been flying with for a long period, associates who had become kind of like family to me. Once I collected myself, I called Independent Air.

Independent Air confirmed the report. I also learned the cockpit crew consisted of the same people with whom I had been flying just about three weeks prior to the crash. It was just one of those things that was almost impossible to believe could happen. After some research to find out everything I could, it appeared that the accident was caused by pilot error, confirmed by a company representative who said the crash happened due to a simple misunderstanding of the altimeter setting.

When flying international, the altimeter setting is given in millabars instead of inches of mercury, which can be very easily confused if you are not used to it. Evidently, the setting was not what the copilot thought the controller said, therefore placing the airplane about 1500 feet lower than it really showed on the altimeter, an altitude, unfortunately, not high enough to clear the top of the mountain. I also saw it on the TV news at the motel after returning from school.

The captain flying the plane had just returned to flying from a couple of months off due to a broken foot. The copilot was new, with virtually no international flying experience, and this factor, in itself, is an accident looking for a place to happen. The captain was quite inexperienced, and we had a hard time getting him proficient enough to pass an FAA captain's check ride.

I remember having some problems with him during some of his training. He would frequently misread the approach plate. I often had to correct and caution him about making the wrong turns that were not depicted on the plates, missing his assigned altitude, and other airmanship faux pas which could cause major problems. He did finally get checked out, and, in retrospect, it was probably a mistake giving him the reins on the big bird for international flying. This same gentleman flew as copilot at Air Atlanta, but the company refused to consider him for the left seat.

On the doomed flight, the captain's fiancé, a young woman of only twenty-two years of age, worked the aisle as flight attendant. The senior flight attendant was the oldest flight attendant with the company. A good buddy and a dependable attendant, she loved to fly. She transferred to our company from Eastern, provided my memory's still intact.

These folks became like family to me. I got permission to leave the class to be able to attend the funeral, which was at Nashville, Tennessee. Virtually the whole company was there at the funeral, along with relatives and friends. It was a very big gathering with a military flyby because the captain was a former Army helicopter pilot and a current reservist.

I returned to the DC-8 class a couple of days later. I hadn't really missed too much and was able to catch up quickly with a little help from my friend, High-Speed Brown. It was just a typical ground school like most of the others with one small exception. The big difference was that we had to go to Stockholm, Sweden, for our simulator training and FAA check. Stockholm is located on Sweden's South-Central East Coast, where Lake Mälaren meets the Baltic Sea. Over 30 percent of the city area is made up of waterways similar to Vienna, Austria, with lots of green parks located throughout the city. We were there in the winter time, so it wasn't unusual for the temperatures to drop into the *bitterly* cold range.

Our accommodations were utterly fantastic, a neat little suburban hotel with a very nice proprietor—kind of a mom-and-pop operation. The simulator was located at Scandinavian Airlines training facility, which was second to none, in my opinion. I never knew or even bothered to ask why the company was using this facility. I assumed it was cheaper or there was none available in the U.S. Nonetheless, it was an excellent location for us to do our simulator training.

High-Speed Harry and I ended up as partners for the simulator training, which would ultimately become the greatest simulator training

I have ever experienced. A real prince of a guy, Harry managed to keep me in a laid-back mode, making the training much easier to take in stride, along with the calm environment in which we found ourselves. We would split the four-hour period and rotate who would go first each night. Actually, I think this was the easiest transition I have had up to this date. Naturally, Harry and I would always have to execute our personal debriefings at the hotel bar while putting away a few jars until the wee hours of the morning. After all, the camaraderie with a few post-flight beers functioned well as an important part of a non-sked training profile. We would also have time to view the beautiful city from time to time, hitting some of the local bars in order to view some of the luscious Swedish ladies.

I don't remember the name of the FAA examiner who came to give us our check rides, but he had also kind of used the trip from the U.S. for the check ride as a vacation for him and his wife. As best as I can remember, he came from Louisiana, which is probably true, because the company's headquarters was located in New Iberia, Louisiana. He and his wife were super people as were most of the folks from that part of Louisiana known as Acadiana. The natives of the area had a cute nickname they adopted—they called themselves "coon-asses."

Harry was to take the first ride, with our company instructor in the right seat, which at that time was the normal way to do it. Harry passed with flying colors, and I entertained no doubt about that. When it came time for my check, however, something happened, and our company instructor would not be able to ride with me, so the company asked the FAA examiner if Harry could ride the right seat for my check. The FAA guy said that it was not a normal way to do it, but in this case he consented.

At one point of the check ride, I was doing an emergency check list with the flight engineer. Harry was flying the airplane as a normal procedure. The examiner cautioned me about having Harry fly so long. I responded, "This is what good captains do to assure the check is completed correctly." He just laughed and said I was absolutely right, but this was a check ride. Because I always felt very comfortable flying with Harry, I, too, made it with flying colors through the check rides.

We then went to St. Louis for our airplane flight check with the FAA. The company had an airplane based there to fly charters to the islands. We could also make use of the aircraft for the check rides. Several other people had also arrived to get their checks. Some made it through the check, but others didn't. The time was so limited that the company had to reschedule some of us for another day. Unfortunately, I happened to be one of those guys, so there was nothing else for me to do but to go home and wait.

I didn't have to wait too long. Gulf Air called to confirm my current status on the 727. The company had a contract with Air Malta carrying tourists to and from areas of Europe on a daily basis, and I was hired for these flights until I could take my DC-8 flight check. I had been hanging around the house too long and was ready to roll. So away I went to Malta, a beautiful little island in the middle of the Mediterranean about fifty miles south of Sicily, 175 miles east of Tunisia, and 200 miles north of Libya. A beautiful place for tourists with an average daily temperature of about eighty-five degrees during the eight months of summer, Malta offered itself as an inviting place to go lay in the sun for a few days, a tropical beverage on one side and a lovely bathing beauty on the other. The coastal waters there were so blue you could mistake them for the sky above, another one of those places on the planet that would make you think you had died and gone to heaven.

As was the case, I went on to meet several pilots from the Air Atlanta program, which recently had closed its doors under bankruptcy. So, as the non-sked business opened its arms to me once again, I said to myself, "I think I'm going to really enjoy this flying." The flights headed to European destinations, but the majority of them flew into England's Stansted Airport in the Northeast suburbs of London. I flew mostly with my friend Kenny Carroll, who worked for both Air Atlanta and Independent Air. He hadn't moved over to the DC-8 program yet. I think he was very content doing what he was doing at this time, which is quite understandable—it was a near-perfect work environment. We usually departed Malta at a reasonable hour in the morning and returned from the UK in time to enjoy a swim and to put down a pint or two of Guinness, probably the best flying duty that anyone could ask for right here.

I had no intention to leave this place in a hurry; however, the call finally came to return for my check ride on the DC-8. This time it was going to be completed in New Iberia, Louisiana, where the company was located. I had never been there before. The company kept its offices on a small airport about half way between Houston and New Orleans called Acadiana Regional Airport. To my surprise, the company operated out of a motor-home-type trailer complete with about three or four rooms, positioning aircraft all over the world out of a small place like this!

We stayed there for a few days, enjoying the deep-south hospitality as well. I got to meet one other captain and a couple of flight engineers intending to complete their own check rides. We mostly hung around the motel pool during daylight hours and in the bar when the sun had set. We enjoyed some great seafood and crab feasts at a number of local restaurants, whose dining tables had a hole in the center of the table with a handy trash can beneath to catch the crab-shell waste. I don't know why it is, but every time I eat those things I have crab parts all over me when finished. I guess it is just part of the meal. I love to eat them anyway. Evidently, the company had difficulties getting an FAA examiner for the check rides, explaining why we had such a good time there. As a result of the day, a couple of the guys impatiently quit and went home. I fully intended to stick it out until I got it done this time.

Early one morning, we got the call that the FAA examiner would show up that day, and we all needed to present ourselves at the airport at noon—an unexpected situation because we all had stayed at the bar until the wee hours of the morning, and I personally was in no shape for a check ride. I pulled myself together, gulped down a handful of vitamins, and headed out to the airport. Among the impatient aviators, the other captain had already gone, so that left me to fly the whole check ride. To my good fortune, the examiner did my check first. Unbelievably, I passed, but I still had to fly the airplane for the other pilots' check rides, which took about two or three hours for the whole ride. One of the flight engineers confided to me later that he didn't know how I passed the check ride in my condition because the final landing I made was not something to write home about.

Gulf Air had a crew that had timed out at Stansted, England. As a result, the company contacted me to fly copilot with Harry Brown and other crew members to relieve the timed-out crew. We were flown there commercial to pick up the airplane and to continue the trip. Our flying agenda included a flight to Madrid, Spain, followed by a flight to JFK for our own crew rest. I was very glad to climb back into the saddle again after the long wait for the check ride. I would have to fly copilot status for a while until a slot for a captain's position opened up. I couldn't think of anyone better to start my line flying with than High-Speed Harry. We also reunited with a couple of our former Independent Air flight attendants, Trixie and Betty Boob, who had resigned after the Azores crash. They informed us that they no longer felt safe with Independent.

After we arrived in England, we discovered that the airplane had a very bad hydraulic leak in the wheel well and that the leak appeared to come from one of the accumulators for the system. This was not a good sign. The passengers were already loaded and ready to go. We had no choice but to off-load the passengers and to assign maintenance to solve the problem. The word we received from maintenance was not good at all. The accumulator had to be replaced, which would take at least another day, due to the fact that it had to be ordered and shipped in from another facility.

The company had no other option except to send very unhappy passengers back to the hotel for another night. Harry called the next morning to check the status of the problem. Maintenance had received the part and was working on the replacement but could not give us a time of completion. To compound the entire situation, there would have to be an additional delay of at least one hour to allow the maintenance crew to pressurize the system before checking for leaks.

Maintenance finally fixed the problem, we reboarded the passengers, and off we flew to Shannon, Ireland, for a fuel stop then on to JFK. Soon after our takeoff from Shannon, Trixie started to check the custom's forms that were needed for our arrival in JFK. She noticed that the handlers at our departure point had not stamped them. This would definitely create a big problem when we attempted to clear customs.

Trixie had been a senior flight attendant for many years and usually could figure out a fix for most any unusual problem. Savvy, experienced flight attendants often played a key role in the success of a flight in the always dynamic world of non-sked charter operations. She went back to the flight attendant station, thought about it for a while, and came back to cockpit with her plan. She said the padlock for the galley in the back was a combination-type lock with an oval circle with numbers in the center, resembling the stamp used by customs. She thought if she rubbed some mascara on the bottom of the lock, she could stamp the forms. We had no choice but to give it a try, so we did. When we presented the custom's forms at destination, we had no problem whatsoever—a "job well done" for Trixie. She deserved at least one free jar at the bar, but I think she got several of them instead.

We checked into the motel for our crew rest, all of us pretty well beat after that long fiasco, and most everyone just turned in for the night. After a little while, I received a call from the company with the request to get in touch with Harry. I explained that the last time I saw him he was going to his room to get some well deserved sleep. The company administrator wanted Harry to get the crew together to fly the airplane to Los Angeles. I responded that I would see if I could round him up. I went to his room and knocked on his door, letting him know who I was, and he motioned for me to enter. As it turned out, Harry *already* knew that "they" had attempted to reach him. Until his crew had rested, he said, there was no way that he was going to take that airplane to Los Angeles. He went back to bed, and so ended that particular story.

The remainder of the time I spent with this company flew by virtually without emergency events or abnormal situations, ironic because non-sked flying would usually be fraught with unforeseen problems. We really enjoyed the relatively uneventful trips.

CHAPTER ELEVEN
THE AMAZING AFRICAN-BUSH FLYING ADVENTURES

Around 1991, I was sitting by the pool at my house at Port St. Joe Beach in Florida, soaking up some sun along with a few beers and watching my adorable wife swimming in the pool, when the phone rang. I answered and found myself talking with an old flying buddy of mine, Lonnie McRae, who was now living in Miami and flying for a company that flew vacation charters. He advised me that he had passed my name to a friend of his in the aircraft parts business in Miami, a fellow who had sold a DC-8 to a company flying support missions in Angola. This sounded right up my alley, so I told Lonnie that I was definitely interested, and I contacted this person.

Lonnie, believing I was the man for the job, informed the guy that I had already done this kind of flying earlier in my career in Biafra. When I reached the gentleman by phone, I learned that I kind of already knew him. I will call this person Sanford because he reminded me of the older Sanford from *Sanford and Son* (of TV sitcom fame), both of whom dealt with the Miami airplane junk yard called "Corrosion Corner," which stored all types of junk airplanes there. Sanford said he had a DC-8 that he needed to get to Angola very soon. After checking on the pay, which I found it to be more than satisfactory, I consented to do the trip. He said, "Thank you very much," and that he would set up the arrangements for me to travel to Miami and would get back to me in short order.

Before the day had ended, he called me with the travel arrangements to Miami. When I arrived in Miami, the company put me up at Ho Jo's on 36th street, where I had stayed many times before. The company made a vehicle available to me for the duration of my stay. Everything I consumed at the motel went on to the company's tab. In a peculiar way, I had so much comfort that I gave momentary thought to cancel out on the trip and to hole up there for awhile. I say this because nobody seemed to have a clue how long it would take the maintenance guys to get this thing ready to fly again.

This airplane was one of the very first DC-8s that were built, a DC-8-21, which was near the first model, I believe. The plane carried the old straight-pipe JT-4 jet engines. The oldest one I had seen up to this point was a 52 model, which had JT-8 engines. After a little more research on this airplane, I found that it had been stored somewhere in Washington State for the past ten to fifteen years. One can imagine things like the condition of the fuel tanks after sitting there that long. For sure, all the seals would have dried out so badly that the tanks would leak fuel. Then, too, all the petroleum fluids would have congealed. When an aircraft sits on the ground for an extended period, nothing but bad things happen.

Another crew had flown this thing to Miami. From what I understood, they had lost an engine en route and had to land in St. Louis to have it fixed or replaced. They finally got it to Miami, where I figured they had cleaned the carbuncles and other unsavory critters out of the fuel tanks to make it flyable again. They were still working on it every day since my arrival.

I enjoyed myself in Miami while I waited. I visited some of my friends I knew from flying the non-sked cargo. I went to dinner a couple of times with Lonnie and ventured into a few night spots (some with topless entertainment) on 36th Street. We were married guys who were not allowed the "hard stuff" that was available in Miami Beach. I never was one for that place—just too fast for me, I reckoned.

After a few days, the maintenance guys said they thought the airplane was ready. The owner had acquired a permit for a one-way deal with no return options. We went to the plane to check it out for ourselves. There were only three crew members: yours truly, the copilot, and the flight engineer. We did not have an augmented crew as would be necessary today, according to current FAR regulations.

The copilot was a good friend of the owner, himself an inexperienced pilot who most likely had never flown a jet before. He had a wooden leg due to amputation as a result of some kind of accident. Initially, I didn't really make his disability much of a concern.

I figured he had cleared through the FAA to get his medical back. The flight engineer was a lot like the son in *Sanford and Son*. He, the flight engineer, of course, worked for the owner, but he had also managed to get a flight engineer's certificate. Consequently, my cockpit colleagues appeared to be a little wet behind the ears.

Once we had approached the airplane with the intention of taking off, we immediately smelled and caught sight of fuel covering the whole ramp area underneath the wings. When we moved closer to inspect under the wings, the fuel poured out like rain. Naturally, we had to talk about this for more than a *little* while because I was not accustomed to flying airplanes that were raining fuel out of the wings.

I found it extremely difficult to believe that the FAA would even *consider* letting us fly this thing. I assumed the airplane problem explained the reason for the one-way ticket: to get this thing out of here before it caught fire and destroyed itself and possibly other airplanes!

The maintenance guys, to add insult to injury, had installed some sort of navigation radio system which they mounted on top of the instrument panel with duct tape! The guy who installed it said that he had a hard time finding an electrical source to connect it to. That's a red flag right away for me. The owner had a couple of maintenance guys hired to take the trip with us, knowing we were going to have problems with this thing on the way. They were the original airplane's mechanics from its point of origin back in the State of Washington.

The airplane was also completely loaded with all kinds of parts, even an old surplus jeep-like vehicle that the owner had purchased from the Post Office auction in Miami. They planned to use the four-wheeled thing as a ramp vehicle at São Tomé, where the buyer's company was located. On top of everything else, the plane was topped off completely with fuel!

We finally did everything we could possibly do and were ready to get on our way. We got our entire flight plan coordinates programmed into the navigation system that was mounted on the instrument panel with duct tape. The owner was brave enough to take the trip with us. He rode in the jump seat behind the engineer's station. I really had no clue what the airplane weighed. We were full of fuel, and the cargo load looked very heavy. I didn't see any weight and balance forms. The airplane even felt heavy during taxi to the runway.

We were cleared for takeoff. I asked the flight engineer to pay particular attention to the engine power after it was set for the takeoff. We started the takeoff roll, the airplane appeared to be accelerating very slowly, but I knew we had a very long runway and wasn't worried too much about that at the time, although it did take an excessive amount of runway to get this thing off the ground. We finally got her in the air and started our clean up procedure: gear up, flaps up on schedule, and so on, based on the appropriate airspeed. Before we even got the airplane cleaned up and the after-takeoff checklist complete, we noticed that the airplane was getting very hot inside the cockpit. In addition, we could hear a loud noise of airflow and some vibration just beneath the cockpit area. I asked the flight engineer to check out the problem and to see if he could get it under control.

Departure control had leveled us off at 3,000 feet until they could give us further climb clearance. The engineer could not control the temperature. I looked back at Sanford and saw that he had already started wiping sweat from his brow. I advised control that we needed to maintain our present altitude and continued to be vectored for traffic separation until we solved a problem we had with the airplane. Control agreed to help us out with this request. It appeared that we were not going to be able to control the temperature. I really didn't have to ask Sanford what he wanted us to do. All I had to do was look at him, and right away he gave me the thumb down, which I knew meant to get this thing on the ground while we could. My copilot with the wooden leg appeared to sit there in a complete daze, so it was all on me to get this thing back on the ground.

We had burned very little fuel, meaning the airplane was about the same weight it was for takeoff, so I knew that we were way over weight for landing. This meant that I would have to make the smoothest landing that I had ever made in my life. Everyone was wet from sweat, and the temperature was getting to the point that it was making us all a little dizzy. I asked the controller to vector us for an approach and landing—that we needed to return to the airport.

I didn't ask for an emergency landing. Had I done so, I knew the problems could only worsen, especially since they had only given us a one-way ticket out of there. After getting on final with the runway in sight, the tower cleared us to land. The runway was kind of blurry due to the sweat running into my eyes along with the dizziness from the overbearing heat. I knew it was all up to me to get this thing on the ground safely under adverse conditions. I was getting close to the runway for touchdown and took a couple of good, deep breaths from the oxygen mask hanging behind me. This mask is primarily used in the event of a rapid depressurization of the airplane, and only takes about three seconds to don. This cleared my vision somewhat for landing. I guess God was with me again because I got on the ground with one of the smoothest landings I had ever made. The first thing we did after landing was to open our side windows in the cockpit, not to let the cool air in but rather to let the hot air out.

We taxied "the thing" back to the ramp from which we had departed and shut it down. Sanford immediately told us all to leave the airplane and to go across the street to Wag's restaurant to wait for him. I knew the reason he wanted us to wait: he would have to dig down deep to find some plausible explanation to the FAA. "If at first you don't succeed, then try again another day," and that was the plan.

After an hour or so sipping coffee at Wag's, Sanford arrived with the news. He said that after discussing the problem with the FAA, we would have another chance to get out of town. I don't know if Sanford had a big pocket book or had connections; it really didn't matter to me one way or the other. As for me, I only wanted to get out of there and on our way. Sanford advised us to check back into the motel until further notice. For beginners, the maintenance people concluded that they had left an electronic-access door open just to the rear of the nose gear, clearing up the mystery behind the wind noise, but we also didn't know yet why the heat went to full hot. Whatever the problems were, maintenance informed us, they would get fixed.

We waited there for all of the next day and into the evening when Sanford advised us that we would be able to leave the next morning. We all went to bed early since we knew we had a long day ahead of us and had no clue of what could possibly go wrong next.

We all gathered at the airport the next morning. There was nothing much different visually—the wings still rained fuel, covering the ramp underneath the airplane. Nevertheless, the guy in charge of maintenance said we were good to go. "Yeah, right," I said to myself. It didn't matter one way or the other—we had gone as far as we could to get this machine in operation, as far as I was concerned.

Our route would take us to Caracas, Valenzuela, followed by Recife, Brazil, then northwest to Abidjan in the Ivory Coast of Africa, and eventually on to São Tomé. We finally got this piece of defecation of an air machine off of the ground and on the way to Caracas. We all looked at each other in dismay, hardly believing that we were *really* on our way. Everyone appeared to be in a good state of mind. We began to relax, even cracking an occasion joke to inspire some laughing.

We made it to Caracas without incident. Because we were not flying under any time restrictions, we decided to journey on to the next stop, Recife. On this leg, I decided I would test my wooden-legged copilot. He appeared to be doing fine, with a little help on the rudder control for the takeoff roll. Other than that, he held his own. I could tell right away that he wasn't too familiar with flying jet aircraft: it was hard to get him to rotate the airplane up to the jet-airplane climb attitude which was different than the old reciprocating aircraft technique. The swept-wing aircraft handles a lot different than the old straight-winged prop planes.

We were about half way to Recife when we noticed the smell of electrical smoke. About the same time, the *fantastic* (intentionally tongue in cheek, of course) navigation unit taped to the top of the instrument panel also went tits up. "Ah, ha," I thought to myself, knowing that everything was going *too good*. We turned this jury-rigged navigation device off and threw it back into the rear of the airplane. We then relied on our other navigation aids for the rest of this flight since we were over land and had VORs to use for navigation. Right now we needed to get to Recife and then to figure out the navigation problem before going across the Atlantic.

My wooden-legged copilot was still doing reasonably well flying the airplane, and we were getting close to Recife. Sometimes it is necessary to lead the controllers in these areas by telling them how you want to do your descent, along with other aspects of the arrival profile. A normal, comfortable range descent is about a three-degree descent rate, which means if you are at 30,000 feet, you would need to start your descent at about 100 miles from the destination airport.

I wasn't really paying much attention to what the copilot was doing at the time, and, when I did look it over, I noticed that we were sixty-five miles out and still at 31,000 feet, which was getting just a tad too close in for a comfortable descent and approach. I enlightened him that he should have started his descent earlier, but there was nothing to do now but to improvise in order to get the airplane down to a lower altitude.

We were getting closer and closer, but we were still too high. I observed that the copilot wasn't going to do anything, so I had to take control over the airplane, to slow the airplane below the maximum gear-down speed, and to put the gear down to make the airplane descend faster to assure we could land on the first approach. It was a struggle, but we got the airplane down on the hard surface at Recife and that was the end of a reasonably successful leg number two.

The two maintenance guys were to stay with the airplane after arrival to try to fix any problems we might have. They were continually tightening screws on the wing panel on top of the fuel tanks, trying to stop some of the fuel leaks. They were also supposed to try to get our *great* (tongue in cheek) navigation system fixed to permit a successful flight across the Atlantic Ocean. While the maintenance crew worked, the rest of us ventured on to the hotel. Our layover hotel was fabulous, situated directly on the beach, with short, dark-skinned bathing beauties all over the place. It was nothing other than a miniature Rio de Janeiro.

We had access to a nice swimming pool constructed in the center of the motel, surrounded by tropical growth and several bathing beauties, and, if the truth be told, a very inviting place to mess up the airplane in order to stay longer. However, I knew Sanford would not go along with that thought. He was still viewing those dollar signs in his head. What he did do though was to treat us all to a very nice Recife dinner with surf and turf and all the trimmings. A few martinis were complemented by a bowl of boiled pigeon eggs, which I had never had before. We were all up at first light the next morning to make our plan for the day. We checked with the maintenance guys to see if our navigation system was fixed. They informed us that it was "fried completely" and could not be repaired. Now it was decision-making time.

I informed Sanford that I had been in this same position before and was able to navigate across the Atlantic by using my ADF radio and the flight chart to get us there. I showed him how I did it by using the radial from the station or the bearing to the station to depict my coordinates and to report them to Oceanic control. This had worked twice for me, and I believed the alternative would work again. Dead-reckoning across the ocean is real easy *if you know what you are doing*!

Sanford and son and our copilot agreed to go for it. Then I suggested that Sanford give the maintenance guys an option not to go with us if they felt uncomfortable with our creative navigation methods. Neither one of them had a problem, voicing, in fact, complete trust that I could get us there based on what they had seen so far. While their vote of confidence made me feel appreciated, I also felt on the spot. We filed our flight plan to Abidjan, with the option of being able to continue on to São Tomé when reaching the half-way point if our fuel would allow. The guys had even got the fuel leakage slowed down to a slow drizzle. So we were on our way again. It was unbelievable and scary that we were not having any *really major* problems! Everything was going *too smooth*. Our two ADF radios were tuned to Flores, a navigation station at the Azores on Ascension Island. With both of them working, we could give a picture of our reporting points, and with the radar we could depict any islands on our flight path.

In the meantime, I found something for our copilot to do as I kept him busy with our navigation and position awareness. This "across-the-pond" flying was new for him. He struck everyone as a real nice guy, who came from someplace in the Midwest, either Michigan or Indiana. When we approached the half-way point to Abidjan, I had to run a fuel check. Taking me off guard, he said he already had made the fuel check, and we could make it with plenty of fuel to spare, based on our current ground speed.

As I looked back at Sanford, I noticed he had heard the conversation and pointed his finger straight ahead. He was very pleased since our progress would save him the additional costs of an en-route fueling stop. I called Oceanic (air traffic control) and told them the plan. They gave us the revised clearance, and we were on our way to São Tomé. I took the radio that was tuned to Flores and switched to

São Tomé. There was no reception at this time, so we continued on our present heading still reporting our positions by the use of Ascension's beacon and the time between reporting points for our ETA.

When we got to a point where thought we were about thirty minutes out, I tilted the radar down slightly so I could pick up the São Tomé Island when we got close enough. Sanford had been around enough that he knew what I was doing and was up on the edge of his seat watching the radar screen and the ADF beacon. In about another fifteen minutes, a patch of white showed on the front edge of the screen. Sanford said, "There it is!" I knew that was it, but just to kid him a little, I told him it was only weather. Then I tuned the radio to the tower and reported in. Tower control responded right away. Everyone, particularly Sanford, was really excited. We had made it across the Atlantic one more time without proper navigation aids!

I asked the tower for descent clearance and was cleared to descend to 3,000 feet. We were still on top of a cloud layer, but I had the island on the front edge of the radar screen. I knew that the airport was on the other side of the island and that I had plenty time to get the airplane down. It didn't matter anyway because we were already there, and it wouldn't hurt a thing to get a little view of the island from above, especially for the guys who had never been here before.

We broke out of the clouds at about 10,000 feet and could see everything below, airport included. I asked the tower if we could circle around for a bit before landing, and they approved. I flew straight over the airport and out over the water and turned left to circle back in for a landing on the south runway—another fine landing by the Bush Pilot to add frosting onto the cake for another successful trip. Sanford and Son were particularly happy because of the payday they were about to receive, for this would be the place where the financial transaction would complete itself.

These São Tomé Island guys jumped right on the plane and started downloading. I knew how these guys operated because I had been here with them back in 1969 when I was flying into Biafra during the country's revolutionary war. They delivered the copilot and me to the company compound for some well deserved crew rest, and that was exactly what I did. It was already about "dark thirty" anyway, and a good sleep would feel mighty good.

I woke up early in the morning before I really wanted to because I felt very sick at my stomach. I didn't have a clue why I ached so. It wasn't the time of year to have a cold, so I jumped back into the sack and tried to return to dream land. But that didn't work. About then I heard some pots and pans rattling in the kitchen and decided to go check it out, maybe even to help myself to a cup of coffee. The cook was there getting ready to put together some grub for breakfast. He invited me to have a seat, and in a short while he would have the coffee ready. After I identified myself to him, he said with a cheek-to-cheek smile that he already knew. Somehow my reputation had preceded me. We then engaged in a little small talk about the trip and all. He was very congenial. I described my stomach problem to him, and he said, "No problem. We have doctor here. He can check you after breakfast."

After I put down the man's breakfast, I went see the doctor. He asked a lot of questions, trying to find out what might be wrong with me. When I mentioned the pigeon eggs that I had eaten the previous evening at Recife, he said, "Ah, ha! Bad eggs! That's the problem." He handed me these small, black pills that looked like little lumps of coal from the West Virginia coal fields. As a matter of fact, they tasted about the same as a hunk of coal. He said I should take two now, two before bed, and two in the morning, then to come back to see him the next day.

I made it clear that I had to fly the plane to Angola the next day. He replied, "No fly tomorrow! Come see me tomorrow." I told Sanford what the doc said. Sanford agreed with the doc and said that I should follow the doctor's orders and that there was no hurry to get to Angola anyway. I could understand that because he and Sanford Son had already collected their money. They intended to continue on with us to Luanda, where they would catch a flight back to Brussels and on to Miami on KLM airlines. Then, too, their maintenance guys needed to check the airplane over some more because the fuel-leak problem still existed.

When the sun rose the next day, I thought I would just tour the island with a couple of crewmembers, since I hadn't been there for about twenty years. Nothing had really changed that much. The washy,

washy women continued to clean their clothing along the river and ocean banks. The town area remained virtually the same. When we arrived at the Hotel Miramar, my haunt back in 1969, I noticed many changes. Now completely renovated, the place had become quite a popular vacation resort. What was most noticeable to me was that the local people had not changed at all. The copilot, who accompanied us on the "Sanford" trip, stopped by to enjoy a couple of drinks. By this time, I began to feel a little better.

When my companions and I finished our day's tour, we headed for the compound to check everything out. The maintenance people said that they were almost finished with the airplane, indicating we could continue on to Luanda the next day. There wasn't much to do here for night life except to go to the Hotel Miramar to drink too much, which, ironically for me, I didn't feel like doing at this time because of my stomach problem. We just stayed at the compound and played poker until we all decided to hit the sack.

Around nine the next morning, a maintenance fellow called to report that the airplane was ready to go, provided we, too, were up for it. We grabbed our belongings and made it to the airport. This was going to be a real easy trip. The only thing left on the airplane was the mail truck and a few parts. The flight to Luanda would only take some thirty to forty minutes. We filed the flight plan and programmed our *new* GPS that maintenance had installed at the same place on top of the instrument panel—except that the GPS was now *properly* mounted with brackets instead of duct tape. These guys were true professionals.

We had no problems on this leg to Angola. It was a beautiful day for flying. I had been to Luanda about twenty years earlier, but now I rode instead of flying. Luanda is the capital city of Angola. When I was there in 1969, one could compare its beauty to Athens, Greece, because, like the Parthenon situated prominently atop a hill, a section of Luanda did the same. The airport had two runways, 27 and 24. The former would handle the length requirements for very large airplanes, such as KLM's 747s.

After we landed and taxied to the arrival gate, one of the company representatives, along with the customs people, met us at the airplane. They gathered all our passports and customs documents, took them away, and left us more or less abandoned on the airplane. We waited there for a good while before a customs person finally came to escort us to the customs check point. Needless to say, we sensed something amiss with our paperwork.

They told us that we would have to wait in the customs area to be cleared for entry into their country. Since none of us could speak or understand Portuguese, we had no clue what was going on. Admittedly, we did harbor a reasonable amount of fear, considering the fact that we had just flown into a country *still* at war. We had no idea whether we would be considered "good guys or bad guys."

The on-going Angolan Civil War (1975-2002) between the Liberation of Angola (MPLA) and the National Union of Total Independence of Angola (UNITA) centered primarily on control of the diamond, jewel, and petroleum riches of the Republic of Angola, and here we were—smack dab in the middle of armed conflict!

Following about one hour in contemplation of either freedom or imprisonment (or worse!), the company representative approached us. He said that there was a problem with the papers. He had called another company person, who could communicate with the customs people to get it straightened out. He also said that from what he knew about these people, they were plainly trying to squeeze out more money from the company. Most airport officials at third-world airports back then were "on the take" if they thought they could pull it off. And this time they did it again.

After the representative showed up with the big U.S. greenbacks so loved by these airport officials, we were released to go on our way. The driver took us to the company office to meet the "CEO" as well as other company employees. They were all very receptive to us, offering us drinks and inquiring about the trip's pleasantries, and so on. Naturally, we did not discuss the trials and the tribulations in getting the aircraft to its destination.

Most of the staff consisted of Portuguese, German, British, Philippine, and American nationals. The majority of Americans had worked as maintenance crews for Southern Air Transport, an old airline company that operated the current fleet of C-130s. Prior to the DC-8s, they were only operating the C-130s and Lockheed Electras. There were only a few American pilots and one flight engineer for the C-130s. The Electra crews were all Filipinos.

Because we would operate without the oversight of FAA or of any other restricting agencies, we could fly without limitations, especially the restriction that confined aircrews to a certain number of flight time. As a result, some of the C-130 crews clocked in over 300 hours per month, flying approximately ten hours a day, seven days a week! Moreover, we went airborne *without* MEL (minimum equipment list) restrictions. It was a common thing to fly with a generator, a fuel pump, or even a radar unit inoperative. Flying with one engine out or with a blown tire was no big thing here either—as you will soon find out.

The company invited me and the crew to stay a couple of days in order to carry out a couple of trips until they could put together a regular crew to operate the plane that we had just delivered. We all agreed to do so. The company would send the maintenance crew home as soon as transportation could be arranged. We were then transported to our living quarters located just outside the city of Luanda on the east side.

Corimba 3 on the Beach

A nice little, two-story building, our new home had a kitchen, a dining room, a lounge, and three upstairs bedrooms. In addition, three comfortable-looking motor homes served as living environments. The cooks were mostly Portuguese and Filipinos. Local people handled the maid service. Completely fenced in, the compound, known as Corimba 3, maintained a security guy there at all times. Frankly, I was not convinced I could trust these guys either. Like the noticeable swollen thumb, everyone here outwardly sought the American dollar.

In lieu of telephones, the place had radios at every location for communications. During our first dinner together, we got the call to prepare ourselves for flying action the next morning. Sanford and son, we learned, would also accompany us to consider the purchase of another old junk airplane that had crashed on landing at the airport. They wanted to determine if the plane could be resurrected. They did, in fact, buy the thing, but it was a long while before they managed to send it to a facility they maintained in Johannesburg.

I was awakened the next morning by this little ding-a-ling Portuguese house keeper, as that was one of his duties today. We all gathered for breakfast. I first tried the coffee, which tasted like it had a half cup of raw coffee mixed with hot water—much stronger than espresso! The food-prep people served up a pretty good breakfast buffet; however, I'm sure the cholesterol content was off the scale on the high side, even though the food did taste quite good. I ate some of the food and talked the cook into fixing a little go-bag for me to take along on the trip.

We then proceeded to the airport, where I immediately noted we did not have to file a flight plan. I concluded that the same trip every morning required no paper work, more or less the classic "kick the tires and light the fires" operation. We stopped by this little trailer which functioned as their operations center on the airport ramp and received our itinerary for the day. We were scheduled to make at least three trips to various destinations with the possibility of another (TBA).

The loading was done virtually in the same manner I experienced years ago in the Biafra flying. Some innovation had been adopted, though, as they were using metal instead of plywood pallets. It was still virtually the same kind of operation: no weighing devices—so again, we had no clue of the aircraft's weight at takeoff. Then, too, we had no way to figure the weight of the black-market contraband that some of the higher ranking people were putting on to make a little self-benefitting side money.

When we pulled up to the aircraft, we again observed the wings continually leaking fuel—although now with a little less accumulation on the ramp. Someone, we deduced, had figured out how to minimize the fuel leakage. Nothing mattered any longer, it seemed, because of the absence of FAA and its regulatory functions, pure *laissez-faire* at its best because we were able to operate without restrictions as long as we could deliver the cargo to its destination and get paid for doing so.

Except for our Filipino loadmaster, we were about to operate now with the same crew that brought the airplane here. None of us knew anything about this operation simply because we hadn't done it before. The GPS installed at São Tomé already had all the routes installed with directions on how to use it with the aircraft. We punched in the first station, the Monongue Airport, located about one hour and thirty minutes distant. With everything programmed and the engines running, we headed toward runway 27—due to the fact that out of the two runways available to us, number 27 had the longest length.

There we were with the aircraft's engines puffing up a storm ready to take off. So far so good. We lifted off the ground, cleaned up, and made a left turn out to about a 150-degree heading, intended to get us on course with the GPS. We were cleared to climb up to our assigned altitude of 32,000 feet. Everything was going *too* smooth.

When we reached about 15,000 feet, the windshield suddenly made a rather loud, disconcerting noise. I immediately observed a windshield covered completely with cracks. If you have ever seen a cracked windshield on a wrecked car, you know what I'm describing. Constructed out of some five layers of glass and plastic, airplane windows are fashioned this way as a form of protection against bird strikes and any other objects that may impact. On the other side of the coin, seeing through such a cracked windshield offers a most interesting challenge.

Sanford and son, along with one other company exec, would certainly have to change their pants when this day had ended! Looking closely at the situation, I concluded that only one of the inner panes had cracked. I wasn't too worried about it then, but proper visibility at landing could certainly pose a problem.

Fortunately for me (and for everyone else on board), I had practiced this particular scenario way back in my flying-instructor days. I knew that as long as I could determine alignment with the center of the runway, I would make use of other references to get the machine on the ground. One particular reference has to do with side vision, known also as peripheral vision, for ground-closure rate. I know it is probably hard for non-pilots to visualize what I am talking about, but, believe me, it will work. I'm sure that lots of pilots who fly in cold areas like Alaska have had to use this technique when their windshields would ice up.

Unable, of course, to do anything about the cracked windshield, we continued on toward Monongue. I overheard the control tower communicating with aircraft tuning them in for the approach. As we neared the airport, I asked the copilot to check in. He called but received no response. A short while later, the copilot called a second time. Still no one answered. A few minutes later, the controller asked, "Did someone call Monongue?"

The controller pronounced Monongue differently than the copilot. As we soon found out, most of these places are not pronounced as they are spelled. He subsequently called back and inquired, "You have breakfast?" The copilot looked at me, asking if I understood the meaning of the guy's question. Considering the request simply a form of subtle bribery, I informed the copilot to say "yes." I knew that the controller wanted something to eat, and for that reason I brought along the doggy bag from our morning breakfast to make this particular fellow happy, for he then allowed us to get priority for landing.

Fortunately for all of us, our altitude during the flight put us out of reach of the war zone's stinger missiles, which had about a three-mile range. The approach to landing was a little different here than normal. We would fly directly to the airport to be over it at flight level 200 (20,000 feet), which is roughly four miles above the airport. We would then slow the airplane down below maximum, gear down speed, and circle down to the runway within three miles of the airport, maneuvers meant to position us out of range of enemy fire.

The controller would communicate wind direction and speed and which runway was in use. Of course, there was no problem of landing on the runway of our choice. We performed everything correctly and got lined up straight in with the runway. I could see the runway, but not really well enough to satisfy my self-preservation instinct with good depth perception. Falling back on the method learned years earlier when faced with a cracked windshield, I put the side vision for ground closure successfully to work—nothing to write home to mom about, but we made it. As all pilots know, any landing that you walk away from is a good landing.

I grew to accept that going to any of the airports on the first flight of the morning could be very dangerous. The war persisted, and no one knew what to expect to find on any given day. It was not unusual to have to avoid holes in the runways and taxiways due to the 175mm rounds that would hit during nighttime fighting. At times we took note of burning buildings, trees, and brush areas surrounding the airport.

Accordingly, we operated on an important rule of thumb: if no one responds to a radio call to the tower, "We don't go there." Inevitably, such non-responses did happen on some occasions, indicating the possibility that the airport had been taken over by the rebels. Sometimes we could even see battle tanks at a distance from the airport during descent!

We made it a habit to keep the #4 engine running in order to have air from that engine to start the other engines. On this particular run, we'd clear out our cargo and prepare for departure. After we put down, Sanford and son scurried off to negotiate the purchase of the crashed airplane while the local military soldiers off-loaded the plane. In the meantime, the hungry traffic controller showed up to fetch his breakfast and stayed with us for a little while. These guys could speak the minimal amount of English required to be an air traffic controller.

The control tower looked a whole lot like a wooden outdoor toilet that one would see back in the countryside hills of Kentucky, greatly resembling the outhouses my own family and I had in the old days when I was growing up. The airport housed nothing except for a couple of what appeared to be Russian-built Mig-17 fighter jets. Furthermore, the airport had no real terminal since the facility served strictly as a military landing field. Its runway was about 10,000 feet in length, long enough to operate the jet fighters.

We got the airplane off-loaded, Sanford and son returned, and we made arrangements to fly back to Luanda. Return trips were normally problem-free because we were empty and very light. The climb out was the same as the landing. We had to do a circling climb to flight level 200 (20,000 feet) before heading eastbound towards home. After arrival and while we sat in the crew bus on the way to the company office, a company rep asked me if I had a resume. All non-sked pilots always carried resume copies in their flight cases. I gave him a copy. We then dropped him off at the company office and proceeded to Corimba 3, effectively ending the day.

The crew and I had nothing scheduled the next morning for us— probably because the maintenance crew had to try to fix the cracked windshield. I did receive an invitation from the director of operations. As I walked into his office, I noticed my resume lying on his desk, easily imagining why he wanted to see me. And exactly as I had imagined, he offered me a job. After he reviewed my resume and found that I was a check captain, including the trials and tribulations to deliver the airplane to Luanda, he declared complete confidence in me to handle the job. To my complete satisfaction, the director offered me a very generous salary. I would not only hold down the previous chief pilot's job, I would also function as chief pilot on the Electra. The company already had a good chief pilot for the C-130, on which I wasn't qualified anyway. I also inherited the former chief pilot's living quarters, a motor home parked, also to my complete satisfaction, adjacent to the pool. My schedule called for two months on and one month off, including free transportation home and one-month salary during the time I spent with my family.

The offer looked too good to turn down. I informed the director I would think it over and let him know the next day. I called my wife that night and explained the offer to her. She really didn't like the idea of me being away from home that much, but she was actually kind of used to it already and agreed that it would be okay with her if that was what I wanted to do. So the next day I accepted the position.

The new position would prove to be a lot different from my usual aviations jobs. All DC-8 crew members, with the exception of one British captain, came from the Philippines. I figured out why the company didn't offer the position to the Brit: he was one of those guys who demanded to do things his way. I put the idea into my head not to worry about this character trait too much as long as he did the job and didn't get anybody killed. He was, in my view, a very good pilot and a gentleman who, like me, enjoyed drinking and sharing war stories. I took pleasure in his companionship, and we got along pretty well together.

All the other guys who accompanied me on the original delivery flight eventually returned home. The copilot with the wooden leg, however, stayed on, evidently because he and Sanford were friends. I learned, too, that Mr. Wooden Leg held shares in the company, somehow persuading the right people to allow him to fly copilot on the Electra. This meant that I would still have him aboard because I was also the chief pilot on the Electra. Although admittedly most of us considered him a really nice guy, it takes more than that to be able to fly under the warring conditions confronting us here in Africa. He did endure for a couple of months and then had to go. If he had been able to fly with me all the time, he would have been all right, but the Filipino captains thought differently.

The company eventually moved me from Corimba 3 *up* to Corimba 1, a very nice compound where all company executives, chief pilots, and all other crewmembers, excluding Filipino loadmasters and maintenance people, took residence. Our new quarters offered nicer homes and gardens, surrounded by all kinds of tropical vegetation, including a small, picturesque swimming pool. A couple of big dining tables sat directly in front of the mess hall under a mango tree, including a screen over the top of the dining area to provide shade. The setting offered a great place to gather with the other guys to discuss all kinds of personal stories and flying problems that occurred that day or over the past week—all the while sipping on a cold beer or nipping on a bottle of Jack Daniels.

Under the Mango Tree—Henry's Hangout

The Tropical Pool and Garden Area

Perched on top of the mango tree, an old parrot named Henry managed to drop his loads with an uncanny accuracy I had never before witnessed. This flying character would hop across the screen until he positioned himself directly over the head of his intended target *(kind of like he was equipped with a Norton bomb site)*. Not only did we have to put up with the excreting antics of Henry, we also had to deal with a couple of monkeys that numbered among the biggest thieves you have ever seen. You could not leave *anything* lying around the mango tree or the swimming pool area.

The "promotion" from Corimba 3 to 1, perhaps comparable to an upgrade from a GI barracks-level setting to bachelor officer's quarters, provided me with my own fridge and cooking stove. I used the latter to prepare pots of homemade bean soup and pones of cornbread, both of which were on hand all the time. Naturally, I used the refrigerator to store lots of brew. The Brit pilot really loved to come down to enjoy the fruits of my labor with me. On occasion, I would invite some of the other guys as well.

Located very close to the beach, our living environment motivated strolls through the sand or frolicking in the waters of the Atlantic. The beach setting also allowed the local black bathing beauties to offer themselves for a reasonable price. I knew that a lot of the guys from the Philippines took advantage of this option, forking out twenty bucks for just about anything they desired.

We did not receive actual currency here. Instead, the company set us up with a direct deposit with the offshore Jersey Bank. However, we could make company draws for any amount of cash we needed, and such withdrawals would be taken out of our pay. A hundred-dollar bill would stretch out a *loooooong* way. Actually, there was nothing much to spend money on (with exception, of course, of the beach beauties) since everything was there for us at the compound. If needed, we did have shopping access to a sizeable British grocery store, which also carried a selection of liquor. I liked to drink orange juice then (and now) and would purchase a case or two. My friend, Jack Anderson, favored Jack Daniels, so I would return with a bottle for him in the luxury of company transportation; after all, I was the chief pilot.

Now all settled in, we'd have to get to work flying the airplanes, and this operation would soon reveal itself as a strange operation. The first problem had to do with a communications break-down between me and the Filipino maintenance personnel. On the flip side, all the flight crews could speak English and Tagalog. As a result, flight crew members translated for me.

The company already had one other DC-8 present, which, of course, also had lots of maintenance problems. None of the fuel gages operated, so the airplane had to be flown by using the time and fuel flow calculations, which was certainly not perfectly reliable, and the flight time to arrive at how much fuel remained in the tanks. Other flight crews had been flying the machine this way already for a considerable length of time, I heard, so I didn't worry *that* much. In addition, the radar was virtually inoperative. Then, too, the antenna would fall downwards enough to point to the ground after anything but a smooth landing, making it unreliable during thunderstorms, regular events every afternoon around two.

On top of all these disturbing problems, the flaps would jump track occasionally and would have to be positioned quickly to the last position to prevent the airplane from going into an uncontrollable, steep turn. The main cargo door, next, had to be *chained* to the closed position, with "come alongs" pulling the door tight because the normal locks had been broken during a previous flight by the Filipino crews. The list of problems areas could go on and on and on. Even then I held the opinion that some of these old, beaten-up birds would make some of the corrosion-corner-tarmac queens at Miami look like keepers! As you may very well imagine, nearly every flight presented several emergency-like situations!

Besides the maintenance problems, we experienced the same old loading problem. The actual weight of the airplane was never known for sure. The only way I could tell was to check the shiny part of the landing-gear strut. If I observed less than the length of a pack of cigarettes showing, we were too heavy. I mentioned much earlier in the book about the type of pallets and rollers that were used. The latches for the pallets were built into the floor of the airplane, which was fine as long as they all worked, but they didn't. Occasionally, one of the pallets would come loose and start sliding back and forth in the airplane. From the on-loading point of view, the soldiers loading the plane moved about as fast as molasses growing on an ice cube in the middle of January in Alaska!

I wondered for awhile why they all had on their field jackets in the 110-degree weather. In a few days I found out. They wore them to be able to steal food from the load on the airplane. These people would literally kill one or the other over a stolen frozen chicken or any other food item. I once observed one of them putting frozen chicken under his coat. He then ran across the ramp. At least four others chased him down, beat him up, took the chicken, and left him lying there on the ramp. A short time later, some other guys came with a tow tug used to pull aircraft. They threw him across the hood and hauled him away. Sometimes, according to other eye-witness accounts, they showed absolutely no forgiveness at all: they shot the thief when they caught him stealing.

Unfortunately, we had no way to control the loading problems. There were so many deals going on between the company and some of the local politicians and business people, allowing just about all parties to load their black-market items onto the airplane, that my crew and I backed off. Under the circumstances, we had no choice other than to deal with the blatant smuggling. Even the air traffic control people personally hand carried things to the airplane. Sometimes they would even *ride along* with their goods to assure a safe passage to the right place and into the right hands!

One of the airplanes was set up for cargo and the other for jet fuel with portable fuel tanks through the cabin of the airplane, tied down with chain and fastened to the floor via tie-down loops. The tanks were all connected together with four-inch rubber hoses and clamps, obviously a potentially dangerous operation that I will explain when we get to fly this particular story at another time.

We were all loaded up on one occasion for our first flight of the day to a place called Huambo, about an hour's flight away. The airport elevation there stood at about 5,000 feet with about a 7,200-foot runway length, which meant that the fully loaded DC-8 had to be flown right on the money with landing and touchdown precisely at the end of the runway to be able to get the airplane stopped prior to leaving the other end and ending up on the grass.

This was my first trip to this airport, so I really didn't know what to expect. We, namely the controller and I, experienced a communications breakdown on the landing attempt. I thought the controller cleared me for one end of the runway. I got lined up on the runway he had assigned. The controller then said I was on approach to the wrong end of the runway, prompting me to go around to land on the other end. I then steered the machine to the other end and made the approach. I knew we were overweight so I added some air speed for the wife and kids and continued my approach.

Similar to landing at the mile-high airport at Denver, Colorado, the trees and the ground zipped by very quickly. At the same time, I gawked momentarily at the short-looking runway, wondering if I would have the good fortune to get this thing stopped. I kept on going, trying to make the touchdown as close as I possibly could at the end. If any animals had strayed near the end of the runway, I would have crushed them for sure, because I was right down to the ground coming across the threshold! I must have put the wheel to the surface not more than fifty feet down the runway! I braked and put all four engines into reverse at the same time, but I still didn't appear to be slowing down enough to stop before going off the other end.

I did everything in my power to get this big, heavy bird grounded, stopped, and rolled right up to a point where I could look straight down to see the green grass off the end of the runway. What I had just now accomplished, I figured, would suffice because the nose gear did perch on the pavement. Nevertheless, I knew I would have to practice some landings, especially when the runway was wet. A couple of the Filipino captains refused to land there under rainy conditions. At any rate, we made it and taxied to the off-load point.

When we reached off-load, however, we encountered another somewhat uncomfortable situation: other airplanes were parked there, so it was a chore to get this thing turned around into the designated spot within the wing-tip-to-wing-tip parking area. Soon I learned, too, that this area was probably the worst place for trouble with the cargo off-load crew, and this day was not a good day regarding the off-load routine because part of our load consisted of booze.

The off-loading went along relatively smoothly up until we heard some commotion in the back. Some of the loaders had broken into the booze. Obviously now totally toasted, they fought over the remaining liquor. About that time, security soldiers showed up to take care of the problem. Before I could decide whether to wet my pants or not, I heard shots from the AK-47s they carried. One of the loaders had grabbed a bottle, I found out later, and sprinted off into the woods. I did not determine if the soldiers had shot the thief, but the shooting and the fighting, thank goodness, stopped.

My copilot, Julius Aquino, a very religious person, quietly sat there reading his Bible during this entire hullabaloo. The return leg, representing a less problematic flight because the airplane could now fly with dramatically less weight, would become his responsibility. Even though the airplane carried less fuel, we never refueled at the out stations except under emergency situation. The fighter aircraft had first choice at the refueling stations.

We experienced a very unusual, uneventful return flight to Luanda. The weather was still clear during this time of the morning. The second trip of the day was a little different. As usual, the weather had gotten worse with the swelling of the normal afternoon thunderstorm activity. Determining where the weather was or how severe it might be was virtually non-existent for this area. To add to the drama, we could rarely depend on reliable radar.

The airplane sat fully loaded and ready to go for the day's next flight to Saurimo, located at the furthest destination from Luanda. Saurimo's airport also maintained the longest runway of all destinations, reaching out to about 11,000 feet. However, the runway was very rough with loose pavement lying all around and not built for heavy airplanes such as the DC-8. Instead, they were primarily built for small airplanes and jet fighters. The runway also had a large embankment at its end point. We did not understand the purpose of the mound, but we would soon find out later just how high it was on a later trip.

We topped out at flight level 320 on our way to Saurimo and turned the radar on due to some dark areas in front of us. We saw a solid return on the screen, indicating that the antenna had most likely dropped down into the dysfunctional position, meaning that the radar would probably not help us today. As we got a little closer and started to feel the effects of the turbulence of the storm, I tried adjusting the radar, but nothing happened, so we were on our own again, trying to pick our way through the worst part of it.

To make matters even worse, the air traffic control had no radar either! In fact, control couldn't even depict the position of the aircraft, creating *another* very dangerous problem, because during these storms everyone was "on their own" and no one knew where the other aircraft were. This, of course, generated the possibility of collisions—a bit of airborne "Russian Roulette" over the jungles of Africa.

In such spine-tingling scenarios, I decided to fly at an uneven altitude, such as 500 feet less than the assigned altitude. This would work fine except when other pilots chose to do the same thing! In actuality, we would on occasion pass close enough to take ear-shot notice of other aircraft roaring by—clearly much *too close* for comfort yet unfortunately SOP (standard operating procedure) when flying in non-radar controlled areas. No one knew if other pilots were telling the truth about where they were or what altitude they were flying.

As this particular flight continued, hail and turbulence—standard ingredients of a mature thunderstorm—struck us pretty severely from every direction in which I turned. Finally, we made it through the bad stuff. Actually, in just a few minutes we again reached clear skies. I continued to pilot the airplane while Julius revisited his Bible.

Julius Aquino

Our Filipino flight engineer, a 5' 6" fellow named Ephraim Alarcon, sported a little mustache. A cool dude if I ever saw one, he would just look at you and smile no matter what was going on or how bad it got. An excellent flight engineer, Ephraim soon became the chief flight engineer. I brought about the promotion because I thought he was the best, and he had the respect of the other Filipino crew members. From then on, with the exception of vacation, he always flew with me.

Ephraim Alarcon

These Filipino aviators probably earned more money here than they could possibly make in the Philippines. Some said that they were kind of like millionaires compared to the locals back home. A few of them described the fine houses they had built, with all the luxuries of the free world, such as homes in the middle-class suburbs of the USA. Most of the Filipino flight crews received their training in the United States. Some, like me, spent time in the U.S. Air Force, picking up aviation experience as civilians as well. They were all very educated people, and I treated them all fairly, avoiding any act of favoritism to anyone.

We got along together very well and became good friends. They would often invite me to their area for get-togethers, such as cookouts or just for a few drinks. They would always have a big pot of "mystery stew" because no one really knew what it contained. I did know that they hunted for the cobras that slithered here and there. On one occasion over Christmas time, they prepared quite a meal out of a goat, considered a delicacy. If they were your friends, they were your *real* friends; if not, they might cut your throat in a New-York minute if you pissed them off. I never had my throat cut.

The Filipinos named the DC-8 that we took over there the Grey Ghost—although originally painted white on the top and grey on the bottom—with black around the engine intake cowling. Because the plane had weathered so much from its open storage for so many years, the entire aircraft looked grey. Except for the number on the tail section for identification purposes, the plane had no other markings.

THE GREY GHOST

Recovered from a bone yard in Washington State,
The airplane for the Angola mission was a retired DC-8.
The inactivity caused many a mechanical issue to repair,
Before the airplane would be deemed safe to be back in the air.

Although checked out, patched up, and judged ready to fly,
It had problems that became apparent as they lifted off into the sky.
When they reached a cruising altitude of 3,000 feet,
The temperature began to rise in the cabin to an unbearable heat.

After a return to the airport, they were back in the queue
With a thumbs up and a "Good riddance!" from all the ground crew.
Hoorah! The saved airplane was back in the air!
The Bush Pilot and the recovered airplane made quite a pair!

The trip was not uneventful; to say it was wouldn't be true,
But they arrived safely at their destination, the captain and crew.
After flying one trip with a Filipino captain to show you what to expect,
You were considered checked out and ready in every respect.

Each mission started at dawn to completion with the recovered DC-8,
The cargo always too heavy and over the maximum weight.

Every assignment was stressful and a challenge and took lots of grit,
As well as technique and determination to do the job and not to quit.

The restored DC-8's windshield shattered on the very first mission,
Making visibility next to nothing in this fractured condition.
It was as if the airplane sensed danger and did not want to proceed,
But the Bush Pilot pressed on and gave the problem no heed.

The incident seemed to confirm what they already knew:
That this was the type of flying they could look forward to.
After a few successful missions, the Grey Ghost got her name;
She seemed to be a talisman for success, the Bush Pilot would claim.

The airplane's grey and white color blended with the clouds in the sky,
And she seemed as determined as the Bush Pilot to be airborne and to fly.
The name Grey Ghost came from the weathered exterior of grey and white,
Which made the airplane look almost invisible when viewed in the light.

They flew high in the clouds to ensure the safety of the crew,
And to be as inconspicuous as possible as onward they flew.
Landing was a challenge as airstrips were undersized and elevations
were high,
But the Grey Ghost and the Bush Pilot *always* gave it a try.

The airstrips were thin asphalt, badly broken and much too short,
Making them inadequate for the large jet airplanes in a modern airport,
Airstrips made for the military fighter jets—not the heavier DC-8,
Which made every landing a challenge, thus tempting fate.

The Grey Ghost's name conjures visions of intrigue and a certain mystique,
But she served the mission well—though outdated and antique.
One must wonder if the Grey Ghost—now much older and often
patched—still soars the sky,
And if she remembers the African-Bush Pilot with whom she used to fly.

– ©Pat Mullins/2012

On one particular trip, Julius piloted the aircraft back to Luanda. We took off, performed our normal climb, and headed west back toward an accumulating thunder storm for Luanda. I reminded Julius of the weather. He responded with a nod that everything would be okay. As we climbed, we could see the dark clouds ahead. I muttered, "Ohhh, crap!" and turned the radar on again, mostly out of habit because I knew the thing would not function anyway. The more we progressed, the worse the weather became. Julius made a slight right turn through a small cloud. Once we had flown past the cloud, a large, clear hole appeared to invite us right through the entire dark, ominous thunderstorm!

"How come when you are flying," I asked Julius, "there is always a big hole through the clouds, and when I am flying, I get the crap kicked out of me?"

"God puts it there for me." Julius responded, and Ephraim and I could do nothing but look at each other in amazement.

We managed to get ourselves back to Luanda with no further problems. The next trip of the day would again bring us to the same airport. The weather had dissipated, permitting a smooth ride with no problems. The landing and off-loading met with no problems, and the return to Luanda was uneventful. We finished the day and made our way to Corimba 1 for dinner and a "toddy" under the mango tree with some of the other crews. Then off to bed we went for a good night's rest, for we knew the next day would likely present more or less of the same conditions. We considered every flight a potentially emergency flight.

The next day would turn out a little differently. We were going to fly the Grey Ghost on a fuel-carrying mission to Huambo, my first of such undertakings. We arrived, picked up our schedule for the day, and boarded the Grey Ghost. She still dripped out a little fuel but not as bad as earlier observations. Everything else checked out okay, so we continued on with the before-start checklist, engine start, taxi, and eventual departure. The maintenance crew had even installed a new windshield, so we could actually see where we were going today! We took off uneventfully on runway 27. We made our left turn out as we retracted the gear. When the gear seated itself in the wheel well, the whole front of the airplane started shaking violently.

We all looked at one another as if to exclaim, "What the f...!" The crew immediately exchanged possible explanations while I attempted to retain control of the airplane. After the gear had positioned itself up, we noticed that the two main gear lights indicated the up position; however, the nose gear indicated that it was still down. I requested the copilot to notify the tower of the problem and to ask for vectors until we could figure out the problem. The airplane shook and rattled, truly a bucket of bolts, but not as badly once we got cleaned up and leveled off.

I asked Ephraim to take a look through the inspection hole to determine if he could spot anything wrong with the nose gear. He came back and said the nose-gear doors did not close, an action requiring us to get the airplane back on the ground. I radioed the tower that we had to return for landing and that we needed to dump some fuel to reduce our weight for a safe landing. We received an okay to return, to dump the fuel, and to call back for landing clearance. Already on downwind from runway 27 at that time, we only needed to extend our downwind leg far enough to dump the fuel and to make a left turn in for landing. Ephraim notified me when we were light enough to land. We shut the fuel dump off and told the tower we were ready to turn inbound for landing. We were then cleared to land.

After another grease-job landing, we taxied to the ramp, parked, got out of the plane to see "What the f..." had actually happened. After checking the airplane over, we found that the nose-gear doors were not connected to the retract-hydraulic actuators. The maintenance guys forgot to hook them back up after servicing the hydraulic accumulator in the nose-wheel well. After all three of us had a little discussion with the maintenance guys, the Filipino flight crew themselves cut loose with some good old-fashioned ass chewing. I couldn't do anything but frown at the maintenance men because I could not speak their language. Eventually, we would lift off again and make our way anxiously toward the next emergency.

First, however, we had to refuel our main tanks. Then we taxied out again to runway 27 for takeoff. On the takeoff roll, the copilot would always call the takeoff speeds at V1, and rotate. Right about the time he called for rotate, Ephraim shouted "Abort! Engine failure!" He then began to pull the throttles back. I grabbed the throttles before he could get them back and insisted, "We are going!" We were already past V1, the go-no-go speed. Because we were holding our own with three engines, I figured we might as well continue to destination where we would off-load the fuel and return light, not the safest thing to do, but hey, what else proved itself safe around here anyway?

After we landed in Huambo, taxied to the off-load position, and parked the airplane, a big, yellow fuel truck pulled up to the left front of the airplane directly under the front cargo door. The loadmaster opened the door and directed the driver where to stop in order to position the hose into the tank at the top of the tanker.

I could not believe my eyes what I was about to witness. The loadmaster undid the cap on top of the tank, inserted the hose, and opened the valves from the tanks in the airplane to allow the fuel to gravity flow into the tank. My biggest concern had everything to do with the fact that the truck was still running, releasing exhaust and heat fumes everywhere around the fuel fumes, creating a very volatile situation! I looked at the loadmaster and he looked at me. He must have known what I was thinking and gave me a thumbs-up and a table-wipe motion with his hand, signifying that the operation would turn out okay.

As for me, I entertained the thought that at any moment this whole operation would explode. Ironically, nothing happened. I reckoned one would have to light this stuff with a match to get it to burn. The loadmaster, moreover, did not put my fear to rest when he changed the hose from one fuel-input opening to another. Still pouring out, the fuel gushed down the side of the truck onward toward the tanker's exhaust, creating nothing but steam.

Once the big tanker had pulled away, I felt extremely relieved. During the entire episode, Julius peacefully sat there with a big grin while reading his Bible—kind of like Bob Marley's reggae lyrics, "Don't worry 'bout a thing. 'Cause every little thing is gonna be all right." Fuel still lay all over the place. We cranked up the engines and got on our way with only three of them in operation. This would ordinarily have been Julius's leg, but this time I wanted to handle the three-engine takeoff and then hand over the driver's seat to him.

We successfully took off, climbed, and cruised back to Luanda. Despite an uneventful flight, I still had questions for Julius and Ephraim about the fuel off-load, seriously concerned not only about the way it was done but also about how much fuel was actually in the tanks. They both assured me that everything was all right and that they had been doing the same procedure for a long time and that nothing bad had happened—so far. They also said I should wait until I saw the way the refueling operation was done at Suarimo before drawing any conclusions. When I fell asleep that night, my mind filled itself with more than a handful of nightmares, because Suarimo turned out to be our next morning's destination.

We awoke early the next morning to begin the next day's assignments. To stray momentarily away from any thoughts about Suarimo, however, I'd like to say that my flight crews and I performed these flying tasks every day, actually seven days every week for two months straight, unless we were down due to a broken airplane. We absolutely did not want to miss any days because we received pay at a good rate per hour for every hour we flew, in addition to the regular salary which varied in accordance with one's status. Because of my status as chief pilot, I earned the greatest number of dollars.

When we arrived at the airport for the first flight to Suarimo, old Grey Ghost still hung around with her wings still leaking. We concluded the fuel leak would not be repaired, and we would just have to deal with it. Mentally, we'd have to set aside her age and her non-existing maintenance schedules over the past years. Nobody seemed inclined to improve the plane; consequently, we continued optimistically to sing those Marley lyrics, "'Cause every little thing gonna be all right." I actually grew to love that song!

We loaded up our cargo of fuel and got on the way. We took off, climbed to flight level 320 as usual, put our feet up, turned on "George," the autopilot, and let the plane do her thing. The big old JT-4 engines whined, leaving a vapor trail behind us to piss off the other side's troops on the ground because we were too high for them to hit us with their hand-held stinger missiles. Other airplanes flying into and out of these airports took occasional hits because they did not have the capability to fly as high as we could. We could see these injured planes on the ground as we passed over. We also observed several old fighter planes scattered around some of the airports. Obvious to us, they had been shot down or had crashed on takeoff or landing then pushed ignobly off the runway into the fields. Some of them resembled the T-6 trainer, which also functioned as a fighter in some instances.

To protect both cargo and crew, some aircraft launched flares on descent to and ascent out of the airport. The Filipino crew members said they could hear the missiles in their head sets when they were fired in their direction. The missiles, they said, made a whistling sound. I never heard the whistling because I never wore the headset. Occasionally, I did see the missiles come up, reach their altitude limit, and fall back to the ground. They left a discernible smoke trail especially visible in clear weather. We also saw the missiles hit the flares a few times, creating quite a Fourth-of-July explosion.

"Do you have my breakfast?" asked the tower guy upon approach to the airport. Because we did not want placement into an intentionally delaying holding pattern, we always carried along an extra breakfast or two. Many flights later, we finally asked him for his name. "My name is Charlie," he said, perhaps revealing a common name in Africa.

On this first landing at this airport, Julius pointed to the embankment at the end of the runway as we flew over the thing. Sticking up there kind of high, it was something you would definitely want to avoid on landing. We touched down and taxied to the off-load area, a truly unbelievable sight. We did not confront a fueled tanker truck but rather a trailer tank removed from the back of a truck and placed on a few staggered blocks for support. Why this thing had not tumbled over already, I could not understand. Deeply embedded gouges at the cement level certainly suggested the thing had already shifted a number of feet previously, but there she sat, resting now on the blocks.

I could barely believe my eyes when I realized how the fuel was going to be transferred from the airplane. Since the airplane sat slightly lower than the tanker truck, fuel would not flow gravitationally. To bring about the transfer, the off-loaders used a gas-driven pump to get the fuel *up* to the tank. I still wish I could have taken a picture of this operation to show the outside world what we African-bush pilots encountered! Picture taking, however, was against the rules there. If you were caught doing so, you would promptly lose your camera—if not more.

They, the fuel handlers, had a rag-wrapped connection rigged to hook our hose to the pump, which itself leaked during the fuel transfer!

I concluded they rigged it to leak purposely so they could catch the fuel in a bucket and take it home to use for heating or cooking. I exited the airplane because I had seen enough and walked down the ramp far enough away to ensure my own safety. If this thing were to blow, I certainly did not want to find myself sitting in the cockpit—despite the attempts of my fellow crewmembers to keep me calm and cool. I distanced myself enough to light up a cigarette. I looked back at the operation and caught sight of one of the military guys puffing merrily on a cigarette standing adjacent to the fuel transfer!

I had never seen anything like this before and still don't believe it to this day. They finally finished the transfer of fuel without blowing up the airplane and everything around it. Thank God! I was just *too* used to the way the Air Force did it—base personnel would *not* attempt refueling operations if a thunderstorm had been identified even five miles distant from the base!

Fortunately for all concerned parties, my crew and I managed to make it back to the comfort of our Corimba homestead for an evening of beer, booze, and barbequed steaks. The gathering included everyone in the company with the exception of the maintenance people who lived In Corimba 2. Despite the availability of alcoholic beverages, we learned very quickly that *heavy* consumption of alcohol would serve us poorly, because we worked every day and had to rise very early every morning.

Like most other gatherings, the British and the Americans would end up together, and the Filipinos would separate into their own group. Generally speaking, conversations stuck to our on-going aviation problems as well as to some small talk. The participants brought along a variety of worldly music that we Americans did not recognize. The company also provided a lounge above the kitchen where we could relax and take in a movie.

That evening the DO asked me if I could still manage to fly the Electra since one of the aircraft's captains took off for a vacation. Although no longer current on the Electra, I indicated that I could fly the thing even after my seven-year absence from the plane's controls. In consideration of all other unsound practices taking place, I figured I'd manage okay. The DO then offered to have me accompany another captain on a couple of flights to get myself up to speed, a good plan, I thought, and I accepted the invitation. In the meantime, I'd make the airplane's manual and checklist available for review before I made the practice runs with the captain.

We sat around and shot the bull until about ten o'clock that night, a little later than normal. You just couldn't stay up late and get up early every morning seven days a week as we did. When we experienced a broken airplane, we would get a day off, which didn't happen very often. The airplane would have to be *really* busted up before no one would fly it.

The next day we were scheduled to haul some cargo in the company's other DC-8. The company wanted me to fly it due to the reports from the other pilots of hydraulic-system problems. On the first takeoff of the day, we realized what they were talking about. About a half an hour after departure on our way to Huambo, we noticed that the hydraulic quantity was decreasing. We continued on while closely monitoring the problem. By the time we reached Huambo, we had lost approximately half of the amount we had at takeoff.

This meant that by the time we got back to Luanda, we would probably have some problems. When we arrived at Luanda ready to make our approach to land, we noticed that the hydraulic quantity had almost depleted. After we got the landing gear down and extended the flaps, we noticed a little roughness in the control of the flight controls but not creating that much of a problem, so we were able to get the old bird on the ground. The steering and braking were also kind of erratic, but we managed to stop the airplane and maneuvered it to the parking area.

We advised maintenance of the problem. The maintenance crew would check it out and try to find the problem, which I figured was the same problem that the other crews had previously experienced. Only when these planes completely stopped operating would these guys quit flying them. The loaders finished loading for the next flight, but maintenance still worked on the airplane.

In due course, Ephraim informed me that the maintenance guys had found and fixed the problem. The hydraulic system was re-serviced, and we should be good to go. Not very optimistic about this situation, I made the decision to take off. We got on our way, and the same thing happened! About thirty minutes after takeoff we *again* showed loss of quantity, a problem in existence for two days now and still had not been fixed. Only "corrosion corner" at Miami International could top this poor maintenance! At one point during the flight, we communicated by radio to let everyone at the office know that the problem continued to exist. Nevertheless, we proceeded to our destination at Menongue, covering further distance than flights to Huambo.

We noticed after landing at Menongue that the quantity appeared a little lower than it did at Huambo, placing us in a more difficult situation. We had no other choice. After takeoff and climb, I notified Ephraim to put the flight controls on manual. I would attempt to fly our approach to landing. The system quantity showed almost on empty at that time. After turning on final approach and headed straight in to the runway, we put the gear down.

The gear went down without moans and groans; however, when we initiated the flaps, they would not go any further than about twenty-five degrees. The hydraulic fluid was gone. I knew we would land very fast with very little flap extension. On top of that, we could not know with certainty that we'd even have any braking after touchdown.

"It's now or never," Elvis once sang, and so we could only hope for the best. We touched down at about 130 knots—about thirty knots too fast—immediately put all four engines in reverse, and hit the brakes. Just as we had anticipated, no braking action occurred. I sat there on the edge of my seat, uncomfortably observing the end of the runway drawing closer and closer.

I suddenly remembered that we had an emergency-brake accumulator, and, provided it had been serviced, it might stop the airplane, although our situation really looked as though we would end up either in the boonies or in the water. I pulled the emergency-brake handle. How unbelievably quickly this aircraft would eventually come to a halt! We heard the loud noise of the tires grinding against the pavement of the runway! The airplane came to a stop, with us in the cockpit hanging out over the end of the runway in front of the nose gear. Promptly, tower control radioed that we had a fire under the right wing. A fire truck was already dispatched. With no concern other than survival, we exited on the left side of the aircraft, avoiding the fire raging away on the other side.

Fearing the tire might also blow, sending shrapnel in all directions, we distanced ourselves as quickly as possible from the aircraft. The fire had ignited as a result of the rubber tires dragging against the pavement. The fire truck personnel extinguished the fire immediately upon arrival. A company transportation van picked us up. I headed directly to the main office, which also housed flight operations. Not mincing any words, I demanded to have the problem fixed before my crew and I would again fly the plane. The bosses listened because the airplane was taken out of service for repair.

A few days later, I learned that the hydraulic leak had been found to be way up at the top of the vertical stabilizer, where it could not have been seen without a cherry picker to extend up that high to find it. My concern for the old, bucket-of-bolts DC-8 diminished when I began to fly the Electra the next day.

When we arrived at the airport the next morning to pick up our schedule for the day, some of the maintenance people kind of looked at me in amazement, not knowing that I could fly the Electra as well. I believed then that communications with maintenance crews would pose less of a problem when I learned that the guy in charge of the Electra maintenance also came from the USA. He had been employed by an airline in the states that operated Electras at one time, perhaps Eastern or Northwest.

I asked him about the condition of the airplanes. He looked at me and smiled. His smile alone told me the answer. He showed me a problem with one of the planes that had a crack on the top of the wing, which was, in point of fact, a fuel tank. You could actually *see* the fuel down through the crack! Moreover, the flight crews continued to fly the monster because nobody could do anything with it there, and maintenance couldn't send it any place for repair. The plane, he said, had flown in this condition for a long time, and nothing had happened.

I appreciated his straight-forward stance with me. The rest of the problems would eventually reveal themselves when I began to pilot the airplane. I had read the checklist to review the procedures as well as I could. I remembered that this airplane challenged its crews to get all the engines started in the right sequence. Functioning as turbo-prop engines, they had two different speeds, one for ground operations and one for flight, with the beta range in between. I asked the flight engineer to start them, and I would observe until I got the hang of it again. He was "an old head" at the Electra anyway, so I wasn't worried about it.

We got the engines started and were ready to taxi. Now it would be my turn to do the work. This thing felt like a little toy airplane compared to the DC-8. While negotiating the taxi, I happened to look over at the Grey Ghost sitting there all alone, appearing to cast a forlorn frown to me. The up-and-down shifting of the props was kind of coming back to me now. Like riding a bicycle, once you learn, you never forget, all well and good, but this was not a bicycle.

We were cleared for takeoff and took the runway. Same as the DC-8, the pilot would increase the power of the Electra, and right away you'd roll. On the big DC-8, the pilot would increase the power and wait for the engines to spool up before the airplane would even start to move. As soon as we initiated the takeoff roll, the airplane suddenly leapt off the ground, climbing toward the sky. This trip took us to a small, dirt-strip airport, situated atop a knoll above a river called Waco Congo. The airplanes were used primarily for the diamond operation in which the company involved itself. The airports were also areas where most of the heavy fighting took place. After we touched down, we could hear gun fire in the distance. Naturally, we hoped that *our* soldiers could keep *them* away from the neighborhood.

Our cargo today consisted of large oxygen and acetylene bottles, in all probability used for the diamond-drilling operation. We made the approach and landing without hiccups. We were able to shut this airplane completely down. We exited the aircraft and enjoyed free movement because the plane came equipped with an auxiliary power and start unit (APU).

Exactly as we had observed at other airports, crashed airplanes and damaged military equipment such as discarded airplane parts and a variety of paraphernalia sat there to rust into oblivion, yet providing a good place for animals to seek shelter. The environment clearly resembled a scene directly out of TV's *Sanford and Son*. The sight actually motivated me to take a closer look at the Electras propellers, which were chewed up pretty bad on the leading edges as a result of dirt, gravel, and small rock that would whip up into the air when we reversed engines during the landing. If the propellers began to show transverse cracks, then we would have a significant problem. I assumed that the maintenance fellows kept their eyes on the props.

The airplane was finally unloaded and ready to go. We got it started and took off in the opposite direction from which we had landed, actually more convenient because we were parked on that end of the tarmac. Due to the limited pressurization, the airplane could only go to about 20,000 feet, right on the border line of clearing the altitude that the other side's missiles could reach.

One of the Electras had fallen to a missile shortly before my arrival. The photos I eventually saw showed that the missile had passed through the #3 engine exhaust as well as the flap. The airplane's crewmembers were in route to Maquela, which maintained a small, grass-strip runway, our next-day flying destination. With the exception of a slight yet noticeable propeller unbalance, the Electra actually flew quite well. The aircraft's engines could be synced manually if anyone wanted to take the time to do so, but on these short flights there was really no need.

The day went by unbelievably smoothly: the weather was very nice for flying and the airplane was running flawlessly—once again a scary reminder since we knew that Murphy's Law would sooner or later rear up its ugly head. Nonetheless, I crossed my fingers and hoped for a good outcome. The Filipino captain accompanying us came along to determine if I needed further instruction or help. We landed back at Luanda, taxied to parking, and shut her down. I invited the captain to remain with us for additional assistance or to depart now to return to Corimba. He calmly picked up his flight gear, thanked me, and left.

While the loading personnel worked to reload the airplane, we retired for lunch. Again, the smoothness of the day seemed too good to be true. I knew something would have to happen. On our next flight out, we carried high-protein food supplies packed on pallets.

Now fully loaded, we prepared to blast off. The engineer got us all fired up again, grounds people removed the chocks, and we taxied to the runway 24, where we were cleared for takeoff. Following a good takeoff, we made a left turn out. The copilot clicked the GPS on and selected Maquela, our destination. After passing through 10,000 feet, the engineer advised that we were not pressurizing, not good because we needed to reach at least 18,000 feet to avoid those death-dealing missiles.

Apparently, someone had carelessly left a door open or had missed something that kept the airplane from pressurizing. I asked the engineer to check the aircraft oxygen supply, which he found to be almost full. At 15,000 feet, I knew would be fairly safe until we got within about forty-five minutes distant from Maquela. We would then have to climb to at least 18,000 feet.

The only option we had other than turning around and heading back was to get on the oxygen from forty-five minutes out for the rest of the way until we reached the airport. I asked the other two crew members if they thought they could handle it. They nodded.

We pressed on to the forty-five-minute point and climbed to 18,000. When my crew members showed signs of dizziness, I had them put on their oxygen masks, deliberately avoiding my own mask until I genuinely felt the need; besides, I didn't want to deplete the oxygen bottle, even though we also carried a number of walk-around bottles designed to last about ten minutes. Hopefully, we wouldn't need those. After about thirty more minutes, I decided to suck up a little oxygen myself—just to be on the safe side. I kept the mask on for only about ten minutes.

"Do you hear that?" the copilot asked, a frightened look absorbing his face. I answered that I had heard nothing. He swirled his finger up, indicating a missile. I didn't hear anything because I had on no headset. Like sitting ducks without wings, we simply sat there—waiting. The copilot then gave the finger down, signaling a now falling missile as well as a very close call.

As the copilot wiped away the sweat from his brow, I got the airport in view. It now looked like we would make it again, to have the fortune of "dodging the bullet," despite the knowledge that missiles could not reach us at 18,000 feet. We were cleared to land after we descended close enough to the airport. We landed on the airport's very short, grass-and-dirt runway—no problem at all for the Electra. We taxied to the parking spot, and the copilot showed me where to park and how the maintenance crew wanted us to park. The soldiers accompanying the crew looked as though they had just been in a fire fight, or they had prepared for one at any time with AK-47s slung over their shoulders—a real war zone. All I had in my mind was getting this thing unloaded and getting the heck out of here.

After we shut down the engines, we could hear the noises of war off in the woods not too far away. The copilot, who spoke a little Portuguese, asked one of the soldiers how far away the fighting was taking place. He said, "About five or six kilometers," which would amount to some four miles, "But not to worry." An easy statement for him to make because I had long taken note of those big holes that the 175mm shells make in the ground, easily imagining what one shell could do to an airplane. During those times in the combat zones, I continually held on to an old combat commandment: "*If the enemy is in range, so are we.*"

We finally off-loaded and set things into motion to put the aircraft into the air, making me very happy. We climbed back to 18,000 feet and got out of town. We enjoyed an uneventful return trip. The copilot flew the leg back. We landed in Luanda without incident.

On the next trip, we headed to Mbanza in the Congo to an airport located smack dad gum in the middle of a village! The runway more or less also served as the village's main street: not only did villagers walk along the runway, but also critters like pigs, goats, and dogs put themselves in harm's way. To let the people know to clear everything from the runway, we first had to make a pass over the runway. To my consternation, we'd usually find ourselves landing on very short final before they would clear, and sometimes they would still be clearing as we were rolling down the runway! Added to all this, one of the army generals had a home here. He'd ride with us back and forth to Luanda. When this character showed up, we observed, all the locals maintained straight faces.

The Electras, unlike the other airplanes, didn't fly every day. Consequently, I returned to the DC-8 schedule for the next day of flights, scheduled this time to fly the fuel carrier to Huambo again. I had heard no more complaints about the airplane's hydraulic system, so I assumed it was fixed. Anyway, we would soon find out.

It was raining a little that morning as we made our way to the airport. The company dispatch indicated that Huambo was free of rainfall at the time, so we weren't too concerned. The airplane was loaded and ready to go when we arrived. We also had a couple of passengers, who would have to sit in jump seats in the cockpit. If we had to transport more than two passengers, they would have to find a place to sit in the back on the cargo.

Sometimes we would have ten or more people—mostly soldiers—wanting a ride. They were usually traveling back and forth to the war zone. I reckoned they had to take a little rest and recuperation (R & R) at home. I have seen some of them so desperate for a ride that they would have given up their AK-47s! We also airlifted a number of diamond dealers, who sometimes tipped the crew members as much as $500 each, a noteworthy sum of money back then!

Loaded and ready to fly to Huambo, we performed the checks, taxied to the takeoff point, and prepared to go airborne. We normally flew at about the same weight every trip with a standard load of fuel on board. Occasionally, a number of *other* individuals sneaked some black-market stuff amongst the cargo, but not enough really to make a difference in total weight.

At this point, I do not mind making my own confession: we, my crew and I, *also* engaged in some black marketing ourselves. Almost every morning we packed away a couple of cases of Coca-Cola, which sold then at about thirty dollars a case. These guys, we soon learned, also loved wrist watches, especially digital watches. It was no problem getting two-hundred bucks or so for a thirty-dollar watch! Hooray for capitalism and return on investment (ROI)!

Getting back to the flight, we lifted off and made our turn towards Huambo. Everything looked good—at least for the moment. The hydraulic quantity appeared to hold its own, and we noticed no other problems. However, we always did have the problem of not really knowing how much fuel we had in the tanks on this airplane, but we learned to live with that state of affairs. We climbed to 32,000 feet, relaxed, and enjoyed the ride for a change.

In the meantime, the Grey Ghost made her way to Menongue with another crew and a load of cargo. We occasionally heard radio communications on the company frequency between ground control and other crew members. We approached Huambo and prepared to begin our descent. The tower reported light rain at the airport. I remembered some crew members telling me that other captains would not land there during rainfall. As for me, I decided to give it a shot.

We got on final about three miles out, and, sure enough, the rain clouds had opened. I intended to bring the airplane as close to the ground and as slow as I could over the threshold in an attempt to touch down as close as possible to the beginning touchdown point. Following my command, Ephraim would throw all four engines in reverse as soon as we touched down.

This airplane came equipped with an anti-skid system that would release the brakes as soon as the wheels start skidding. I knew from past experience that, if I did not firmly hold the brakes but rather gave them a light-touch technique, braking would work better. We touched down at the beginning point. Ephraim put the engines into reverse, I immediately used my braking technique, and the airplane really started slowing down very nicely. Only a couple of times did it start to skid, so I just let off of the brakes momentarily until it stopped. We were very close to the end of the runway when we stopped. I even got a big smile out of Julius that time. He appeared to be very pleased with the fact that the airplane did not dart into the jungle. We taxied back to the ramp, off-loaded the fuel, without getting blown up, and headed back to Luanda.

After takeoff and in the climb, we listened to a radio conversation that no aviator, either past or present, would want to hear. The Grey Ghost and her crew had met with an accident in Menongue. We understood there may have been survivors, which, obviously, had us thinking the worst. Once the radio traffic had slowed somewhat, I attempted unsuccessfully to reach the company.

In a short while, however, the company called me back with the news that ole Grey had hit the off-load truck and damaged the #2 engine. Her crew came through the mishap in better condition and requested a pick-up, in due course carried out by one of the C-130s in the area. We went back to Luanda for the next load of the day and fetched our waiting lunch. The truck that Grey Ghost hit had a habit of its engine stalling while backed up to the airplane for loading. Normally, when the offload was finished, the loaders had to push it away from the airplane to let the airplane taxi out.

The incident also meant that we were now down to one operational airplane and not enough flying for two crews. We would either have to split the trips or have someone—or some people—go on vacation until the airplane was fixed. After landing in Luanda, I went to the office to confer with the DO about this problematic situation. He had no answers at the time, he would have to think things through, and he'd get back with me later. Unable to do or to say anything else, I left his office.

Later that evening, he came to Corimba 1 to meet with me. He had two options for me at that time: sending the maintenance guys to Menongue to fix the aircraft there or trying to fly it back to Luanda. The first option would be very expensive, and he didn't know any way we could get it back to Luanda. He asked me for my own input, and I let him know I would need to think about it for a while. I took the next day off and yielded to the other flying crew.

No sooner had I begun to think about solving our dilemma, when the name Jack Anderson came to mind. Born and raised in Charleston, South Carolina, Jack served in the same USAF C-141 squadron with me. A talented flight engineer and a good friend, Jack would have a wealth of knowledge, I believed, to bring our problem to a conclusion. So, together with a full bottle of Jack Daniels, the two of us met in our little Garden of Eden there at Corimba 1.

Jack and I sat under the mango tree, keeping an eye on Henry the parrot, of course, so he wouldn't crap on our head. Yes, we shot the bull, but we also earnestly exchanged ideas on methods to solve old Grey Ghost's problem—our out-of-action DC-8.

Perhaps midway through the bottle of Jack Daniels, Jack described a solution he believed might work sufficiently enough to put into action. The damaged engine, he said, weighed about 6,000 pounds. If we put that much extra fuel weight into the #2 fuel tank, located directly over the engine, such an addition might alleviate the weight-and-balance predicament. We would then have to cap all the fluid lines, Jack went on, going to the engine, disconnect all the electrical wiring, and pull the circuit breakers, leaving us to worry about the large, open hole left by the vacated engine.

I then put my own mechanical abilities to work. If we used pliable sheet-metal pieces to cover up the opening, I figured, we could also make use of high-speed aluminum tape, much like the tape used for HVAC systems, to hold her together. Jack thought it over then nodded, adding that the method would probably work just fine. In the non-sked cargo world, good old duct tape is also referred to as "500-mile-an-hour tape."

All things now considered, I decided we could do it. We'd turn the old Grey Ghost into a "three-holer" (as we call a Boeing 727) since we would attempt to fly her without the number 2 engine. I'd then have to find a crew crazy enough to do the job with me. I knew we would require two captains on this little escapade, so the Brit captain, Patrick Skinner, came to mind. If the money were right, Pat would happily accompany us. I had no difficulty persuading flight engineer Ephraim into going along.

Next came the negotiation. I informed the DO about the plan to fly Grey Ghost home, and we'd perform the feat for a fee. I all but bit my tongue when he quoted an amount far greater than my expectation. Compared to the cost of flying airplanes and parts back and forth every day to fix her, the man's offer most likely represented a drop in the bucket for the company.

I returned immediately to Corimba 1 with the news of the negotiation. Both men also could not believe their ears. We would *all* celebrate a big payday this month. When the Filipino guys found out what we intended to do, however, they did express their worry. Would we practice the job on a simulator? I chuckled and said no simulator could teach a crew how to accomplish what we had set our minds to do.

That night we actually had the chance to sleep in because the C-130 we'd fly would be ready by about noon the next day. We'd take along more parts and an air-start unit. After the morning breakfast, we headed for the airport. Some of the guys continued to question whether we still intended to carry out this crazy plan. Patrick, the Brit, shot them a smile and said, "Well, I guess we are pretty much committed now."

Loaded and ready to go, we waved at the crowd of guys assembled to see us off. The looks on their faces alone suggested they were making a final good-bye to us, and, under the circumstances, not a pleasant feeling for those of us aboard the C-130.

My old friend Bonzo von Haven captained the Hercules for the trip to Menongue. Bonzo, an old-time pilot from a small town near Columbus, Alabama (can you imagine an Alabamian named Bonzo von Haven?), had been shot up pretty bad just a couple of months prior at Benquela, Angola, one of the remote airports that we used. One of the guys who liked to come to my place to enjoy a free bowl of homemade bean soup and corn bread, this fellow could tell a good story or two.

Bonzo got us on the way. It would take a little longer to get there on the Hercules because the airplane flew considerably slower than the jets; in addition, the plane did not take well to higher altitudes. The maintenance guys on board continued to ask about our plan to come away with that big, old DC-8 with one engine missing. Despite explanation and detail, they only shook their heads. Bonzo, I noticed, did not shake his head in bewilderment, for he himself, I was certain, would have attempted the same recovery effort had I been absent.

We landed at Menongue and parked the Hercules adjacent to the Grey Ghost in order to off-load all the equipment as efficiently as possible. When I exited the plane and walked over close to the Grey Ghost, she appeared to smile at me (I kid you not). On the flip side, I imagined her quite pissed off because I had quit flying her and had broken the engine on purpose. The maintenance guys there had already carried out the sheet-metal work, and, resembling a massive bandage, had wrapped "500-mile-an-hour tape" around the entire "wound." Finally, we were assured that the fuel tank for missing engine #2 carried the additional 6,000 pounds of fuel to offset the weight of the displaced engine. She looked *very* strange with one engine missing though, reminding me of someone with only one arm.

Grey Ghost's #2 Engine lying on the ground

Almost patched with 500-mph tape and ready to go

Much like the crowd that had gathered at our departure from Luanda, we chuckled yet cherished the moment when we witnessed the number of personnel gathered to see us off from Menongue. Some may even have positioned themselves to watch us crash on takeoff. We had no intentions of giving them that kind of show.

Because we did not want to put others in jeopardy, we didn't bring along a load master. As we boarded the airplane, I stopped at the entrance door and patted the fuselage a couple of times, as if to sweeten our relationship, "Take us home one more time, baby." Sensing my own pride *and* nervousness, I then claimed the captain's seat.

Patrick, the Brit, sat in the right seat. I began with a briefing, rehashing with Grey's crew members what we had planned to do, allowing each of them to agree or to disagree, since their butts also hung out there on the line. The plan called for me to line up on the runway, and, when ready to go, I would advance power on #1 and #4 engines, start the roll until we got enough speed to control the yaw of the airplane, and then bring in the #3 engine. I also intended to leave the flaps up in order to reach a faster speed at which time I would then put the flaps into the takeoff position. My co-fliers totally agreed with the procedure, which, so far, was working well. In fact, I could not really feel *any difference* with the #3 engine shut down.

THE AMAZING AFRICAN-BUSH — FLYING ADVENTURES

I lifted the Grey Ghost off the ground. Her performance convinced me that she really *wanted* to get up and go! We pulled in the gear on schedule and initiated the flap retraction on speed just as normally as we would have done on other trips with four engines in service. For now, all went well. After we got her all cleaned up, Ephraim said that the landing-gear doors had not yet closed completely.

"Let's give 'er a little more time," I advised him, because we now operated on only one hydraulic pump as a result of the missing engine (the DC-8 had one pump on engine #2 and one pump on engine #3), now providing much less pressure. We continued our climb, hoping the doors would eventually close and lock. Once we approached 18,000 feet, I opted to level out there until we could get the doors closed. We then turned off any hydraulic-powered systems that we didn't need, but, alas, to no avail. We then agreed to fly all the way at 18,000 feet with the speed below maximum landing-gear speed, which was 210 knots per hour.

As you would expect, flying at this speed would keep us airborne over a longer period, but at least we would get there, even though we had not *stopped* hoping. The Grey Ghost had dependable fuel gauges, so we could establish how much fuel we had on the airplane; however, we could *not* burn the additional 6,000 pounds of fuel we carried in the #2 tank. We called Luanda about thirty minutes out and advised that we were on the way in. They already knew our situation and informed us that we would be first to land on arrival. "Nice guys, eh!" exclaimed Patrick.

We lined up for approach and tower cleared us to land. This should not be any problem at all, I thought, unless we had to make a go around. Everything turned out beautifully for us so far. We put the gear down and got our coveted three green lights. Flap extension worked successfully, and all I had to do was land. This would certainly add up to the smoothest approach we had experienced in a *long* time. Of course, I wasn't used to flying this thing when it was light, so I had to make some adjustments here and there. I made a touchdown that was so smooth it was scary. Patrick looked over at me as if to mutter "Asshole"—a common cockpit response from the "pilot not flying" when his colleague made one of those silky-smooth, "grease-job" landings. We taxied to the ramp to meet the gathering of observers there to greet us. I'm sure they had never seen a DC-8 taxi up with one engine missing.

From that point on, it was party time. The DO took us all to the office, broke open a bottle of champagne, and so began the celebration. Although we had succeeded in fulfilling a dubious adventure, one had to fall back on the old saying, "All's well that ends well."

Since all good parties must eventually come to an end, we'd now have to get back to work. We had one airplane down and not enough airplanes to fly. Now would be a good time, I reasoned to myself, to administer crew check rides required once a year in order to hold to an operation resembling a real airline. As a matter of fact, check rides could even make our operation reasonably safer. Then, too, the administration of check rides would allow at least one other captain to stay without loss of any pay. The DO approved the plan. I also had to fly as fill-in for the Electra captain, who was still on leave. We did things this way for at least a couple of weeks.

The time rapidly approached for me to take a vacation. I would first have to find a replacement. A fellow named Bill Stotts came straight away to mind. For some time, Bill, with whom I had flown during my employment with Air Atlanta, had been trying to get me to bring him over to join the company. A laid-back fellow, an excellent pilot, and a highly regarded friend, Bill could surely handle this kind of operation. The DO agreed to get him on the way to take part in our operation. Bringing Bill over, however, would take at least a couple of weeks. For one thing KLM arrived only once a week. Acquiring a passport would also eat up time, and he'd have to obtain the necessary immunizations.

I continued flying a rotation between the DC-8 and the Electra, keeping maintenance wondering which one I was going to fly each day. Those guys always worried whenever I boarded the aircraft. They knew I had a pretty good knowledge of aircraft systems. As a consequence, they could not easily hide anything from me. To all intents and purposes, they actually started to fix *more* of the maintenance problems.

By way of example, the DC-8's #3 engine vibrated at certain RPMs, not a good sign. When the vibrating problem began a good while back, I reported the issue to the maintenance people. Even after they claimed they had resolved the problem, the gosh dang thing *still* vibrated. We pilots commonly commented amongst ourselves that maintenance had "pencil-whipped it": instead of using tools and replacement parts, maintenance performed repairs purely with a pencil. The usual written response was "ground-checked OK."

On one occasion, the vibrating problem worsened. When we returned and parked the airplane, I asked for a ladder that would position me up to the engine's tail pipe. I crawled into the tail pipe and looked closely at the turbine wheel, which clearly had two turbine blades completely missing and a few more with transverse cracking. That was enough for me—without any doubt a very dangerous situation. If this thing blew up, the explosion could possibly obliterate the entire wing, as though struck by an incoming missile! I sent Ephraim to engage in serious dialogue with the maintenance supervisor. We headed for Corimba 1, requesting Ephraim to call us when the maintenance crew had *properly* finished the job. I had no doubt even then that my maintenance-wise disposition as well as my in-depth understanding of aircraft preserved a number of lives.

The next trip I made on the DC-8 was very interesting, a cargo-hauling trip to Saurimo. The cargo load appeared to be very heavy this time—more than usual. They had the pallets full, with extra cargo stacked up to the ceiling. The struts, understandably so, were also very low. I knew we were about to experience an exciting trip. We also transported a couple of passengers—air traffic controllers. One of them, a beautiful young lady, struck us like a Janet-Jackson look alike representing some wonderfully pleasant "eye candy."

The takeoff was one of those roll-to-the-end adventures, not leaving much of the runway left at liftoff. It was a good thing we didn't lose an engine as we did in many instances. We did get it off the ground and started our climb. The DC-8 flew fine once we had retracted both gear and flaps. We proceeded to climb to 32,000 feet and were on our way. En route we experienced no problems—a fine opportunity for the copilot to make small talk with the pretty lady all the way. The weather was severe clear; on approach to Saurimo, however, we were told to expect some strong surface winds across the runway.

The winds in Africa at the time could often blow very erratically and unpredictably with rapid changes in direction and velocity, often creating a swirling effect, which could easily cause problems on landing. We cleared for landing and headed toward approach. As we got a little closer to the ground, the wind began to knock us around a little, requiring the use of full power due to the weight and the cross wind. It suddenly became really hard to keep the airplane straight with the runway, and it started falling. I added almost full power to try to get the flying machine to level off in an attempt to make a smooth landing, which did not happen. As a result, we slammed into the earlier-mentioned embankment with the main landing gear.

The airplane hit so hard that everything hanging on the ceiling, including oxygen masks and other pieces of equipment, came flying loose in the cockpit. We bounced at least ten feet into the air as I attempted to exert control in order to prevent crashing the thing onto the runway, ultimately producing a very nasty scene.

Finally, I set the thing onto the ground, and, at the same time, interior dust blew wildly throughout the cockpit and the cargo area. Once we got slowed down, we opened the side windows to release enough dust to negotiate a safe taxi. The little lady passengers, visually frightened, couldn't talk for a while and most likely had wet their pants. As for me and my copilot, we certainly came close to putting a deposit into our own underwear.

I had to blame myself for this one because I should have kept more airspeed on the approach, which I did teach all the time to the new pilots. Two of the most often-used aviation clichés' are, first, "Keep a little extra airspeed for the wife and kids," and second, "The only time you have too much fuel is when you are on fire."

After the dust settled, we taxied to the ramp. I asked Ephraim to go outside to see if we had any problems there. He came back with his usual grin and gave us the thumbs down: #2 and #3 engines hung down. I went out to take a look and saw that both engines were much lower in the front than usual, with the front of the cowling buckled on both them. Ephraim and I put our heads together. He believed we could still fly with such a scenario, adding that the situation had already happened with another airplane at Huambo. The pilots, he said, had successfully flown the airplane back to its home base but with only *one engine* in the droop mode.

Provided both #2 and #3 engines remained intact, I surmised, we could do the job, even with one missing engine. We always had to take a chance, and I knew I would have to engage in the *smoothest* flying I have ever done before, avoiding any drastic moves with the controls.

We were off-loaded and ready to go. The little ladies stayed behind, presumably either visiting relatives or friends or simply too scared to continue with us, offering a slight advantage because the airplane would now weigh a couple of hundred pounds less.

On the taxi outbound, I hit the brakes very hard a few times to see if the engines might come loose. Nothing happened. So I figured we had a go. I tried to make as smooth a takeoff as I possibly could. We lifted off the ground with no problems. Any change in the configuration of the airplane could make a difference, so we did everything very slowly and deliberately.

Everything went well so far. We did not experience any disconcerting vibrations or controllability issues. All we had to do now was to fly smoothly and to hope there would be no turbulence on the journey. To our good luck, we made it back to Luanda without any further problems. We had already radioed the company, spelling out our situation with the drooped engines, but for company officials just another day of Angola flying.

"Are you ok?" the DO asked. I assured him that we were all fine. He then all but ordered me to spend a day or two poolside, a fine R & R, I thought, because I really needed a day or so away from the stress of near-death situations and severely overworked flying conditions. We now averaged nearly 250 hours of flight time per month. The FAA would have had a field day over here, especially with the 3-engine takeoffs, which became a common thing. If this were a U.S. air-carrier operation, the FAA folks would have worn out their pens writing up violations. We very rarely made a flight without some kind of challenging maintenance problem. I believed that the C-130 guys were experiencing the same thing, but it seemed that they just didn't tell anyone.

The C-130 crews really chalked up the hours. Some of them were probably flying over 300 hours per month. Fly slower, get more time.

They also did a lot of nighttime flying, which allowed them to accumulate more time. As for me, I preferred to pilot the jets and to fly at higher altitudes, where I felt safer.

The chief pilot for the C-130s was an American as well, perhaps a former Southern Air pilot, who already had been flying dangerous missions for several years. A really nice guy, he and I enjoyed each other's company, often taking walks together when we lived at Corimba 1. About the only other place to frequent was a club where the Brits hung out. I went there sometimes with our British captain, Patrick Skinner.

Bill Stotts, my piloting replacement, finally arrived, and I could then take off on vacation in a couple of days. Before I departed, I had to administer his check-out. One day after his arrival, we took off on his first check-out flight and headed for Menongue with a full load of cargo in the Grey Ghost, which maintenance had pretty much restored. I figured this would amount to an easy day for me, considering that Bill would carry out all the flying functions. I had already explained most everything to him about the loads, the fuel, and the condition of the airplanes. I could read the disbelief displayed all over his face, but we continued on. I knew that he would have no problem handling the airplane, but I still needed to get him exposed to some of the emergency situations. Along the way, I also explained descent procedure, approach, and landing.

Most of the things, I deduced, he would learn as he went along—a drastic form of OJT amid the other side's missiles and weaponry attempting to shoot down the airplane while the airplane itself seemingly gasped for its own survival. Bill sat slack-jawed in amazement as I described this radical operation.

The first touchdown in Menongue, thankfully, resulted only in a blown tire, nothing unusual and pretty much a common happening. We taxied to the ramp to off-load the cargo, Bill's next lesson. I explained that we normally kept a spare tire in the cargo hold. To accomplish a tire-and-wheel change, we needed to position the airplane over a hole in the ramp or to elevate it high enough to make the change. One way or the other, we first had to complete the offload.

Almost as though a gift from heaven, an incoming 175mm shell provided the occasion to use the resulting crater suitably as a tire-changing station. The flight engineer jumped out and directed Bill to the opening. We set the brakes. The flight engineer, the loadmaster, and I proceeded to change the tire while Bill watched.

We installed the replacement tire and prepared to get under way again. Bill kept insisting that he had somehow caused the tire to blow. In response, I had to inform him that such an occurrence would happen again and again. All things considered, I thought he had done a fine job handling the aircraft. I flew the rest of that day with him. With the exception of a number of every-day, miscellaneous nuisances, Bill's first check flight went by fairly smoothly. His actions convinced me he had put a good feel on the operation. On a second check ride, we flew together on a fuel-delivery trip to allow him to familiarize himself with that kind of operation as well.

The next day I headed home for a much needed vacation. I had been scheduled on KLM to Brussels, Belgium, and then on to Atlanta following a short rest in a hotel at Brussels. After I set foot into the warmth of home, I unloaded my luggage, pulled out about $10,000 in hundred dollar bills, threw them up into the air, and told my wife that we were going on a little vacation. Most of this money came from the diamond-dealing passengers we transported.

We just happened to have this time-share thing, which would allow us the new-fashioned comfort of a nice cottage in Gatlinburg, Tennessee. We spent the entire week there and really enjoyed ourselves with outstanding luxuries and amenities all included.

I hadn't been home very long before I received a piece of very distressing news. One of the C-130s had taken a missile hit and went down, killing the entire crew. My good friend, Jack Anderson, lost his life that day. The incident touched me very deeply because, as we sat there under the mango tree at Corimba 1 not too long ago, Jack had helped me figure out how to fly the Grey Ghost home with one engine missing.

After I completed my month-long vacation, I called the company to set up transportation back to Luanda. They advised me that one of the company's airplanes was in São Tomé undergoing some maintenance as a result of another accident. I received no elaboration on the accident. To make matters convenient, the company asked me to hang loose at home until the airplane was ready to go. I would then fly to São Tomé, pick up the machine, and fly it back to Luanda.

The hanging loose lasted at least a couple of additional weeks when I received the call to go. Because my wife heard the news about Jack, whom she had met and liked, she verbalized unhappy thoughts about my return to resume those dangerous flights. Nonetheless, I traveled via KLM to Brussels. When I attempted to board KLM's next flight to São Tomé, I was advised that there was some kind of problem with both passport and visa; consequently, I could not board.

Left with no other options, I returned to the hotel to figure out my next move. The only thing that came to mind at that time was to call my old friend in Miami, Sanford, from Sanford and son, to determine if he had the influence to fix the problem for me. Sanford advised me to stand by at the hotel. He'd do his thing and ring me back. In an hour or so, Sanford called to explain that he had straightened out the passport and the visa "misunderstanding," assuring me that I would be able to catch the next flight to São Tomé.

I took a cab to the airport to board my scheduled flight, routed first to Abidjan in the Ivory Coast of Africa and then on to São Tomé. I arrived in São Tomé, checked into Miramar's one and only hotel, an oasis during aviation adventures back in 1969, and called the company to let them know I was there. Again I had to sit tight until the company notified me. I then spent the next few hours putting down a couple of jars at the hotel's bar in the knowledge that the company would pick up the entire tab. After a few days there of chilling out, enjoying the pool, and relaxing in the lounge, the time came to go back to work. The airplane was ready to go—so they said. The company sent along a couple of guys to fly the airplane back with me, in fact, a couple of new guys with whom I had not yet flown. The flight engineer, Sonny Brinkerhoff, came from Texas, and the copilot originated out of the Philippines. We arrived at the airplane, looked it over from front to rear, and agreed that the flying machine looked very good, even with its brand-new tires, which certainly would not last long once we resumed the Angola flying operation.

Bill Stotts, who filled in for me during my vacation, stayed on for a couple of weeks before he was scheduled to go on vacation. Another

Filipino captain would then take his place. The Electra captains were both there, so I would be flying the DC-8s only, unless one of the pilots had to leave for some reason or if I would need to give a check ride.

I picked right up where I left off—flying every day for ten hours each day, seven days a week. The problematic conditions, moreover, remained the same: engine failures, hydraulic system failures, along with the usual problems of flying without a generator, fuel pump, and many other maintenance challenges common in this operation. Both DC-8s were up and running at this time, but one never knew how long that would last here.

About a week after Bill left, one of the Filipino captains experienced another very hard landing at Huambo, effectively breaking down the #2 engine on the other DC-8, putting the aircraft out of commission for a while, and again reducing available flying time—and income. About that same time, the D. O. asked if I would like to take another leave to pick up a 727 in Miami and to fly it to Angola. Since the offer sent musical chimes booming up my spine, I agreed. The plan called for me to get in touch with Bill Stotts, Steve Rodriquez, and three more new hires qualified on the 727 to handle this new mission with the new airplane.

As was customary in this business, I had to wait by the pool for a few days until I could board a KLM flight that would take me home. When I got home, I relaxed and enjoyed the serenity of family life until they called me back to duty. They also extended Bill's vacation until the 727 was ready.

A couple of weeks later, I got the green-light call and headed for Miami, where we all gathered—me, Bill Stotts, Steve Rodriquez, Ken Windsor, Dan Sinclair, and Jose Carara—at the Ho Jo's on 36th Street to wait. We would soon pick up an old Flying Tiger 727, said to be in pretty good shape; however, we found out otherwise later on. I don't think this one was purchased from Sanford and son though. Someone had delivered it to Miami for the sale and title change.

Who originally owned the aircraft did not really concern us anyway. Our concern centered on one question: would it successfully fly? After about two days, we received notification to take the 727 to

Africa. We took receipt of the flight plan together with the GPS navigation system, returned to Ho Jo's, and loaded our coordinates.

Our route brought us first to Barbados, on to Lagos next, then to Luanda. Steve Rodriquez and I planned to complete the first leg to Barbados. Bill Stotts and the other copilot would take charge of the next leg to Lagos. The airplane was pretty well loaded with aircraft parts, food stuff, and various miscellaneous items of cargo. The loaders here in Miami were pretty professional and had the weight very close to correct. For those of us with African-bush-flying experience, to know the actual weight of the aircraft was almost a rare phenomenon.

At any rate, we were on our way to Barbados. Everything was going very well for a change, and we anticipated no problems. The GPS appeared to be right on, comparing it to the VORs, until we left the coast. From there on to Barbados, we flew what we called check-point-charley navigation with Oceanic Control. We put down at Barbados with no problems. The company guy who accompanied us paid all bills with cash, normal procedure for this kind of operation.

On the next leg to Lagos, Steve and I figured we'd have an opportunity to relax and to take a little nap. When I felt my ears popping during descent, I awoke, knowing that we were getting close to Lagos, realizing, too, that the airplane was pressurizing. We landed, loaded her up with fuel, and prepared to take off again.

To complete the flight from Lagos to Luanda, the four of us would split the responsibility. Steve and I flew the first part. As my partner and I were going through the before-start checklist, the company guy prompted us to hurry up with all procedures for departure. He was noticeably jittery, which puzzled me. We got everything disconnected from the airplane and were on our way. However, the guys on the ground motioned for us to stop while the company guy insisted to keep on going!

The traffic controller, evidently not aware of the attempt to halt our departure, allowed us to taxi out and to take off without a hitch. In short order, however, air-departure control ordered us to return in order to pay for the fuel! The company man simply signaled to continue onwards. Who was I to question this man's evident authority? Whatever ensued, I would not lose any skin off *my* teeth.

When we reverted to the next controller, he, too, ordered us to return. Again, the company guy thrust his index finger forward. Finally, we got far enough away that they just gave up on getting us to return to Lagos—chalked up as a nice chunk of money for the company guy! I did learn later though that the company received a number of threatening letters demanding what amounted to a sizeable payment.

About half way to Luanda, we switched pilots as planned. Bill and Ken took it the rest of the way, again with no problems, except when the airplane started a right turn off course due to incorrectly set coordinates, a minor problem immediately corrected. The company man, whose pockets still weighed heavy with cash, explained the reason why they needed the 727. It would fly to some of the smaller airports, he said, that needed supplies, and some of the airports maintained very short, dirt strips they believed the 727 could handle for incoming and outgoing flights. Since I stuck then to the Missouri motto, I'd really have to see this to believe it. We reached Luanda and were checked in to Corimba 3, the beach-front environment in which the big wigs resided. I guessed we were about to receive some special treatment for a while.

This maneuver to upgrade our housing, we reasoned, would attempt to provide us with a little more incentive to fly to the small, dirt-strip airports. We also concluded that the bosses would eventually move us back to Corimba 1.

I really liked our new digs for at least three reasons. First of all, the cook prepared large prawn shrimp along with his special dipping sauce, a five-star-gourmet-restaurant-quality meal. Next, we enjoyed beach access as far as the eye could see. Finally, we gathered at a couple of little beach joints where we refreshed ourselves with cold beers.

The locals did a lot of net fishing along the beach. There was always fish lying on the beach still in the nets drying. The locals would also catch some prawns, including a host of other marine critters. Steve even had the local guys build him a small shack on the beach just down from Corimba 3. Constructed out of palm tree limbs and tied together with the tree's own bark, Steve's "villa" served as a nice place to camp out and to lie peacefully on the beach, setting aside, at least temporarily, the dangers that we all encountered day to day.

Now that we had the 727 at our command, we all jumped even more enthusiastically into the flying mode with the new airplane heading to airports and operating routes normally flown by the C-130s or the Electras. I believed that the 727's speed promoted greater interest on the part of the company, whose representatives always touted, "Time is money," a concept from which the company did not deviate. As long as the company made the dollar, all was fine.

I dare say now that today's pilots would most likely not believe that the 727 could be maneuvered to land without tragic consequences onto small, dirt-strip airports, most of which were strictly military airports, housing only a small shack to provide shelter for the radio operator and his equipment for the very limited information that we received. Consider, too, that the operators constantly gave us incorrect weather information. Moreover, we never really knew the actual wind direction for landing, understandably creating significant problems for these short runways. Even though the landing strips extended out to the 5000-foot-long range, a few knots of tailwind versus a few knots of headwind made a considerable difference in the amount of runway required to stop the big 727.

The new guys would have an opportunity to experience their initial flight with me to Lucapa, a dirt-and-gravel-surface airport with about 5,500 feet of landing distance. To make matters more challenging, I brought them along on a night-time mission, and night time in this area of conflict was *truly* night: totally dark, not even lit up by the lights of nearby towns. From the airplane's point of view, the least little bit of light emitted from the flying bird could be spotted from the ground.

I made doubly sure that my flying companions understood the necessity to keep the airplane's lighting systems as dimly lit as possible. As soon as we started the descent, we turned all outside navigation lights off and dimmed all cockpit lights as much as possible but also to be able to read the flying instruments. I then advised the flight engineer to switch on the landing lights as we came close to the runway for landing. Once we got the airport in sight, I would try to make the approach to the runway the shortest distance I possibly could.

While I cannot now speak for other captains, I had my own way of approaching these airports. We also performed this approach somewhat different from the daytime approaches: we didn't *go over* the airport to start the descent. This happened to be a very clear night, but it was still hard to see anything on the ground.

Finally, we got the runway lights in sight. We would normally come in on the east side of the runway, making it easy actually to choose one runway over the next. On this approach, I optioned to make a left turn in to the runway. I rolled out on final approach about three miles from the runway when the copilot reading the check list said, "Gear down. Three green lights." The engineer, however, presumably only heard "lights" and turned on the landing lights! At that time, all hell broke loose! In an instant, the sky lit up with tracers from the other side's AK-47s! The entire scene resembled a fourth of July fireworks display. "Go around!" yelled the copilot. "Hell no! Turn the lights off!" I replied. "I am putting this thing on the ground *now*!"

If we went around, the enemy's weaponry would certainly attempt to knock us out of the sky. After landing, we inspected the airplane for bullet holes. Although we did locate a few, we did not believe we would lose any pressurization. Then, too, there on the ground we could cloak ourselves in the darkness of night.

"The enemy's getting pretty close tonight, no?" I asked one of the soldiers who spoke some English. "Not enemy. Our guys are drunk. It is Saturday night you know?" he responded, a cheeky grin spread wide across his face.

I then did not simply ask the soldier to stop the guys from shooting at us: I told him! He assured me, along with another broad grin, that he would take care of the problem. To everyone's good fortune, I never heard of anyone getting shot at again so close to the airport. My traveling companions, however, inquired whether they, too, would have to encounter similar close calls. "You haven't seen anything yet," I answered, their heads swiveling sideward in disbelief.

Our departure out of Lucapa, in comparison to the arrival, was pleasant and uneventful. Auspiciously, the pressurization also held up pretty well on the return trip. If we could persuade them to do so, the maintenance people would fill the small holes from the AK-47 bullets. We had one more trip that night back to Lucapa, and then we were off until the next night. Bill and his crew were flying the day missions.

After completing the final trip to Lucapa, we went back to Corimba 3 to put down a couple of cold beers, sitting by the beach, watching and listening to the night-time excitement generated by the local people in the party mode. Especially noisy on the weekend, the jungle music blasted out so loudly that many of us had difficulties to sleep.

Since we were off during the day, we had opportunities to check out the city a little bit. Sometimes we had access to company transportation and other times we would just go up to the road, flag someone down, and offer some money to take us wherever we would like to go for the day.

About the only shopping goods available were the black-market items that were usually located out of town, like on a beach or at a large, open area. You could find almost anything there—if you wanted to take a chance on buying it. Food items could be purchased, but I personally avoided buying any of the "mystery meats." I did buy a few relics, such as wood carvings and other similar objects. We could also find batteries and some hardware items that might be needed for future repair work. For the most part, we simply toured the town, stopping, naturally, to investigate the offerings of small bars open for business.

On one occasion, my exploring accomplices and I discovered an old, abandoned Russian passenger ship that ended up on the docks just out of town. The ship actually had a very nice lounge as well as rentable living quarters. Those who could afford the price, namely the elite people, made use of the ship's environment as a hotel. We, my buddies and I, just happened to fit into that group because we had lots of money with no place to spend it.

Steve and I sometimes spent entire days there. We'd enter the lounge, slap at least $200 onto the bar, and tell the bartender to set up the house until the funds had ended. The bartender knew that we could also pull out more cash if necessary. He also knew we'd leave behind a generous tip.

My drinking pal and I even entertained the notion to spend an entire night there; we never actually got around to do it. As an enticement to spend an overnighter there, however, a number of pretty nice-looking members of the opposite sex frequently patronized the place. Perhaps some of the younger guys went for it, but this dude did not allow such thoughts to enter his head.

Anyway, dark thirty quickly approached for us to relieve the other crew for our night trips. When we arrived for takeoff duty, we noticed our airplane's entire tail section engulfed by a reddish color. When we got closer, we could see the red-clay mud that had splashed all over the section during engine reversal upon landing.

I suspected the situation could damage the compressor blades in engines #1 and #3, namely the pylon engines on the side of the fuselage. The maintenance guys explained that there were some rough areas on the leading edges, indicating that was not the normally expected wear. The problem, I thought, could possibly decrease the engine thrust since the guide vanes were actually air foils—just like the wings—to create lift. Transverse cracking, I reasoned, could also take place, leading finally to engine vibration and possible failure.

I discussed this predicament with Bill and the other flight crew members. We figured we could alleviate the problem by reversing only the #2 engine. We also found a couple of holes at the bottom of the flaps, easily caused by small rocks leaping up from the runway on landing, as the flaps were extended at that time. The maintenance fixed the holes with "band aids," that is to say, with metal high-speed tape used for patchwork repairs on the aircraft's "skin."

We tried the reversing procedure with the #2 engine on this night of flying. The course of action appeared to help considerably. Because we had rainfall that night, we washed off the mud once we had located a couple of areas of heavy downpour, working much like a drive-through car wash without the necessity of quarters.

From the mechanical perspective, we concluded that the 727 would function pretty well. Nonetheless, we still had to guard against "speaking too soon," because anything could happen at any time here in the jungles of Africa. When the 727's tires began to wear out, for instance, our flights would have to be managed differently. Since the 727 does not have as many tires as the DC-8, moreover, we probably could not take off safely with one tire either blown or missing. But, hey, we'd most likely take the chance anyway when caught between that proverbial "rock and a hard place." Although a forgiving aircraft, the 727 could not be flown *too distantly* from its limitations, for she'd bite you on the butt very quickly.

Our next flying adventure brought us again to Lucapa. When we got close enough to contact the ground controller, he warned us of dense fog and calm wind. He cleared us to make the approach and to land. He also wanted us to radio him once we had set down, as though he really did not expect us to land successfully that night.

The runway's rotating beacon just happened to be located directly at the airport. We descended to about 3,000 feet above the airport. We could actually make out the runway lights from above, but that didn't mean that we could spot the lights when we got on the approach in the fog. We were going to give it a shot anyway, so we got on approach on a heading we thought would bring us straight in to the runway.

We continued to descend on final approach. At about 1,000 feet above touchdown, we looked for the lights. When we did not observe the lights, we dropped down to 500 feet—still no lights in sight. I knew it was not too safe to go much lower than 500 feet, but I eased it on down just a little after the copilot said he saw the lights. I, too, observed them, but I believed we were too high to put the airplane on the ground.

At the same time, the copilot thought the same thing and kept pulling the power off, a normal procedure. Ordinarily, he would distinguish the runway, would know we flew too high, and would automatically pull the power back in an attempt to get the airplane lower until the engines settled down to the idle position. This would be okay on the Electra, but it is a dangerous technique and something you never do with the jet engines. If you had to make a go-around, it would seem forever to get the engines spooled up, and that's exactly what happened on this approach.

When I realized we were not going to be able to make it, I called for max power for go-around; however, by the time the power increased enough to stop the sink rate, we had descended even lower. Before we were able to arrest our descent, we were flying through the treetops. The bottom of the aircraft scraped along the tops of some of the local houses, knocking their roofs off. On top of an already scary situation, loud scratching and banging noises accompanied this pulse-racing scenario.

At this point, I truly believed we would soon meet our maker. I even whispered a private prayer or two. My prayers must have been effective because all of a sudden the engines jumped to full power! We began to climb and the noise dissipated. I flew the thing out of there, totally unaware of the aircraft's damage or of what to expect if I attempted to make another approach for landing.

Since I still managed to exert control over the flying machine, I chose to go in again. God must have been watching over us that night because on this second approach the fog had dissipated to some extent, but enough to make out the runway lights from about 1,000 feet. We touched down, thank God, with relative ease.

After we parked the airplane, we hurriedly climbed out to check for problems, and, needless to say, we found many. Tree limbs hung virtually everywhere—in the leading edge flaps, in the landing-gear doors, in the landing-gear assembly, and even in the wheel well.

In terms of equipment to rid ourselves of the limbs, we possessed a crash ax on board. I had a Swiss Army knife, the kind with a built-in saw. The crewmembers had personal survival knives. Impressed? We then put ourselves to work clearing the aircraft of all that unwanted merchandise. In the meantime, the ground crew performed the unloading operation.

We finally cleansed the craft of loose limbs and house parts, thinking the old, battered beast would fly again. Off-loading had nearly come to completion. Soon before liftoff though, a crowd of upset locals showed up looking for the pilots and the airplane that either damaged or removed the roofs of their homes. Shoot! Even today most people, if not all of them, do not take it lightly when a flyboy pilots his big jet plane through their bedroom! We had to think fast on this one.

The loadmaster, a Filipino who spoke some Portuguese, talked to the angry homeowners. Evidently, his words convinced them enough to believe that *another* aircraft had customized their homes. We watched as they then headed for the airport's attendant. Meanwhile, we fired up the engines and took off as quickly as we could.

Once we were airborne, the loadmaster said he explained to the unhappy citizens that an aircraft that had just taken off just prior to our own departure had probably caused the damage to their homes—a good loadmaster with a gifted tongue, a yarn worthy of a case of beer, even a bottle of whiskey, and a steak dinner, an airplane "war story," indeed, that everyone on board could tell the kids and grandkids for many years to come.

After a couple of weeks, we made a shift change. I would fly the day flights and Bill handled the night flights. The two copilots wanted to continue where they were, so copiloting Steve stayed with me. Steve, always fun to fly with, was an excellent pilot, and he pretty much found humor in everything. Considering himself a really cool dude, he thought he had the capability to become a captain. Therefore, I authorized him to fly his own legs in the left seat following a few days of operations.

Our routes changed somewhat for the daytime flying. We flew primarily to Angola's Dundo and Lucapa, with an occasional trip to a number of other airports. Dundo had a *paved* runway constructed out of very thin asphalt—although very rough on the ends, probably the result of heavy-load landings on hot summer days. All in all, the landing strip still resembled a road more than a runway.

Dundo was usually the first flight of the morning. I always got a kick out Steve's radio personality whenever he called Dundo's control. "Dundo, Dundo, are you there? Dundo, Dundo, Dundo. Wake up. It's breakfasssssst time." He spoke his words with such flair that I could never hold back my own chuckle. Steve, because he spoke a little of the local language as well as some Spanish, could actually communicate with the locals. As for me, I learned through Steve that there were some major differences as well as a number of similarities between Spanish and Portuguese.

I could always count on Steve to wheel and deal with these guys. By way of example, Steve once showed an intense interest in buying an old fighter plane that looked something like a T-6 with a radial engine. He actually considered bringing it back to his home in Georgia. Although he finally got the seller to go down to $350, he never found a way to get the thing out of there.

Because of Steve's communications skills with the natives, he managed to remove us unscathed from several embarrassing situations. On one occasion, for instance, we delivered a load of cargo to the wrong airport. The guy who owned the cargo accompanied us. We landed in Lucapa and pulled up to the off-load point. When the owner realized the mistake, he went berserk on us.

The owner, a very big guy, could easily rip us apart if he really wanted to do so. Right away, Steve jumped headlong into the problem, explained the situation, and finally calmed him down, at least to some reasonable degree. With so much weight aboard, we could not take off from this particular airport. We'd have to remove about half the load and transport the remaining cargo to Dundo, the intended destination, where we'd attempt to refuel and head back to pick up the man's other half of the cargo. The mistake would wind up consuming a good portion of our day, but, as the saying goes, "Bigger mistakes will be made." At the very least, we made a regular-paying customer happy. If we hadn't had Steve along, no one knew what the airport screw-up might have "cost" us. Perhaps a limb or two of our own?

While flights with the 727 proved far less eventful for us in terms of emergency situations, we earned less money as opposed to flying the DC-8s. We had only one 727 and two full crews, consequently reducing each crew's flying time to about one-half. Since I would be going on vacation very shortly, I did not worry too much about the loss of flying hours. Soon I'd resume my laid-back position at home. However, I did spot the hand writing on the wall when I learned about the company's plan to hire some local Angolan pilots, whom the company could employ at a much cheaper rate. Clearly, from the company's view point, they'd save the money spent on expensive airline tickets to send us Americans back and forth to work.

I went home, settled comfortably in the couch, and enjoyed some very well deserved R & R. In the meantime, I received a company check every two weeks from the Jersey Bank of London. Without worry and concern, I reverted to a mode that said, "What! Me worry?" We also used the expression, "Mill-around-check-list time."

Despite my worry-free attitude, I still found it difficult to acclimatize myself, for I had grown accustomed to a unique life style there in Africa: pulling myself out of bed before daylight, lifting the air machines into the sky by dawn, anticipating the next missile strike, engines quitting on the takeoff roll as well as other challenging, heart-thumping scenarios that I actually now missed! I sensed I had passed through a freakish thunder storm and had broken out to the other side into complete calmness. But what happened to my adrenalin?

CHAPTER TWELVE
"FINALLY, OUT OF AFRICA!"

Emery Worldwide Airlines

Sometime in 1994 I got a call from one of my buddies from our earlier days with Air Atlanta. He now worked for Emery Worldwide Airlines in the freight-hauling business. He advised me that Emery was hiring at the time; if I had an interest, he'd put my name into the hat. At the time, I did not know if I could resume flying in Angola. On one hand, the thought to return to Angola tempted me. On the other hand, my wife cast a very convincing no-go vote.

Over the next couple of weeks or so, I relaxed and thought. A telephone call to the company operating in Angola revealed that the company's operations had slowed down. In addition, the company continued to make use of the lower-salaried Angola pilots. However, when I heard the words, "Just sit tight for now. We'll get back later with you," I put two and two together and decided to forget Angola and to accept employment with Emery, provided my friend would add my name for consideration.

I really needed to get recurrent on the DC-8 and the 727 because Emery operated both aircraft. I called my buddy to advise him of my decision. Several days later, Emery invited me to join a new-hire class that would begin in about a week. I would resume duties in the same old non-sked business that I began several years back. This time, however, I would fly better maintained airplanes, ultimately making a significant difference with respect to the safety-and-stress factor. The ground school, a recurrent program, would take about two weeks. The simulator training would encompass about two weeks as well. I already possessed a type-rating on the DC-8, so I only needed a check ride. I met again with a couple of new-hire fellows with whom I had previously flown; as a result, the class kind of resembled a reunion.

We finished the training and were sent home to stand by for further scheduling for the line check. I was going to check out as copilot first until a captain's slot opened up—fine with me because I needed to ease back slowly into this kind flying. Following the Angola experience, I knew Emery's work would eventually become very mind-numbing. Then, too, I'd have to fly by directives, maintaining altitudes, obeying controller's instructions, and following FAA rules, all of which fell by the wayside there in Angola.

From the simple, philosophical point of view, one sometimes had to do what one had to do. In many respects, the Emery position would be a lot like learning all over again. We would even be required to maintain a pilot's flight log. After making lots of mistakes, I finally got through the check out and was turned loose to go fly the real world as a non-African-bush pilot.

My first in-the-air assignment with Emery headed to Germany, a country I had not visited for almost ten years. By this time, the two Germanys, East and West, had unified. Emery had a military contract to carry cargo to military bases. Operating on a typical non-sked basis, we set down first at Bitburg Air Base, a front-line NATO base from 1952-1994. We anticipated a rest stop there, but the parking ramp was full, and we had no place to park the airplane. We'd have to off-load the cargo then fly to the next station for the crew rest. We refueled the aircraft and headed to Rhein-Main Air Base, a familiar environment because I had spent about fifteen years flying in and of there with the Air National Guard back in the '60s and '70s. My wife and I also vacationed there for a week a few years earlier.

The flight crew and I stayed at a downtown Frankfurt hotel for the layover, allowing us to tour the city. For those especially interested, I made reference to the city's *Kaiserstrasse*, a street long noted for its numerous bars and its red-light district. I also brought up the possibility of a place called The Pink Pussy Cat, situated interestingly enough right in the middle of town in an old hotel-like building, which housed female beauties displaying their wares at the doorway of each room, much like the *Dreifarbenhaus* (House of Three Colors) not too far away in Stuttgart.

Legalized brothels have been common throughout most of Europe for ages now. As for me, I held no interest, of course, in this kind of activity. In the event the guys wanted female companionship, I simply pointed out where they could please themselves. In addition to the numerous brothels there at *Kaiserstrasse*, the neighborhood provided less costly strip-dancer joints for those so inclined toward sensually visual pleasures. After all this glitter and clamor associated with red-light districts, some of us decided to turn in for the night. A number of the younger, *hungrier* fellows, however, stayed with it for a while longer.

Following the layover in Frankfurt, we prepared ourselves to head back to Dayton, Ohio, to resume work in the freight-hauling business. Although I managed to put myself into the swing of things, I would wake from a nap thinking I was still in Angola. Furthermore, I did ironically encounter difficulties acclimating myself to flights without having to deal with all those bush-piloting problems. This Emery-Air Freight flying, exactly as I had predicted, bored me stiff.

Some of the guys eagerly inquired about my flying days in Angola. After a number of narratives, I wondered whether they actually believed my accounts, for had I not lived to experience Angola, I might very well not have believed it either—especially the fictitious-sounding story about flying the DC-8 with an engine completely missing.

Throughout all this boredom, I maintained contact with some of the other guys I had flown with before. They were working for a new start-up company called Private Jet Expeditions (PJE), flying MD-80s, glass-cockpit-type airplanes that I had never before piloted. The flight management system (FMS) differed from any airplane I had flown up to this point. I was used to what were called "steam gauges." The MD-80 came equipped with "new age" instrumentation, differing as well when compared to the 727.

Private Jet Expeditions (PJE)
People Hauling

Around the end of 1994, PJE offered me a position. Although I hated to leave Emery as a result of the company's own expense to get me recurrent, a number of my flying companions with Emery prodded me to look after myself in this kind of business: if I wanted to make the change, then I should do so; as a result, I quit Emery and joined my next employer.

PJE's training class took place in Atlanta, a breeze for me since I would not have to hole up in an out-of-town motel. Throughout the entire training program, I stayed at home. The program involved an upgrade for me and would require a lengthier period of training—not a problem though, especially considering the fact that I still drew Angola income through the Jersey Bank.

Most of the class members consisted of ex-Eastern pilots already "typed" in the MD-80. A former Air Atlanta buddy named Gil Ramsden tipped me off to the company and sat next to me in class. I didn't really know whether PJE took me on as captain or copilot; frankly, I did not care, overjoyed with the opportunity to put my hands on this innovative air machine.

The systems phase of the training typified any other airplane systems. The avionics, on the flip side, differed, but I was able to get a pretty good understanding of this aspect as well. After about 120 hours, we closed out this phase of the training and concentrated our thoughts on simulator training.

The company originally planned to use the Delta training facility. Evidently, the simulators were busy or the cost was out of range. We then struck out for Minneapolis, Minnesota, to complete the simulator training, smack dab in the middle of winter. Because of the hot and humid and rainy conditions in Africa, I all but forgot wintertime weather in the United States. My classmates and I were about to experience one of the worst winters ever for that area, the Upper Midwest. During the course of one evening, we experienced a record snowfall that blanketed the ground at something like four inches per hour! When we gathered for breakfast the next morning, the snow had accumulated about half way up the windows!

Of course, the motel vans transporting us to the simulator-training school could only inch along, thus prolonging the training period. On top of that, the training facility was situated a long distance from the motel out in the country, well off the beaten path. On the brighter side, I did imagine the grassy pasture fields, the wild deer roaming the fields and woods foraging for food, the birds busily building their nests—a beautiful place to hang your hat *if you could be there during the summer season*!

The simulator training offered us nothing new, but the airplane itself was completely different. The push-button and turn-knob procedures did challenge someone like me, an aviator pretty much programmed to fly mostly by the seat of his pants, a life-saving ingredient in the art of flying in the African bush. I had a very hard time adjusting to the significantly different techniques required to function in the cockpit of this MD-80. For the first time in my flying carrier, I felt like I was sucking hind tit to everyone else, particularly since most of the other pilots had been previously exposed to the newer systems.

Rick McCune, another buddy from the Air Atlanta days, served as one of the class instructors. He continually coaxed me to hang in there. Eventually, he also recommended me for one of the alternate captain slots that would soon come on line. However, something in me had changed during the course of the simulator training. Had I grown too accustomed to flying the non-restricted Angola stuff? Did I lose interest as a result of my now ripened age of fifty-eight? Wherever the explanation might lead, for the first time in my career I failed to upgrade to captain—although I did fly awhile as copilot. I could not help thinking that I had let Rick down, considering that he had recommended me very highly for the position.

On one particular flight out of Chicago early one morning, I flew copilot with one of the ex-Eastern pilots who had just finished upgrading to the left seat and was flying his first trip as captain. We lifted off and found ourselves in very bad weather. This leg belonged to me. I had all the knobs turned and the buttons pushed correctly. All of a sudden we lost everything that had anything to do with the auto-flight system.

The captain, displaying an anxious facial appearance, didn't appear to know exactly how to handle the situation. As for me, I could not now count the number of times I had flown this kind of fly-by-the-seat-of-your-pants scenarios.

"Let's go ahead and try to fix the problem. I'll fly the airplane," I stated, "and you can fix this thing." We didn't have a flight engineer on this airplane as we did on the 727. Normally, the engineer handled these problems for us, but the captain himself would have to see us through this incident.

Once he determined I would capably handle the flying, he relaxed and set himself to work out the problem. In short order, he restored the automatic systems, and we continued on our way without any deviations from our flight path or our assigned altitudes.

I always enjoyed flying into the Chicago and Atlanta ATC environments. These air-traffic-control people, in my opinion, were made up of the best in the world. I was actively flying out of Chicago when the Air Traffic Controller strike took effect. Traffic separation became so problematic at times that pilots had to put up with very long takeoff delays, which, of course, made the passengers very restless and actually created more fatigue for the flight crews, effectively reducing the safety factor. Tired pilots were and are much more prone to making mistakes and crashing airplanes.

I have never held anyone responsible for my misfortune not to upgrade to captain. Rick McCune and all the others gave me all the help and opportunity in the world to do so, but now I guess for some unknown reason the upgrade just was not meant to come to fruition. Maybe it was just like all the times I could have departed the world by crashing in the jungle while carrying out the bush-pilot-flying assignments. It just wasn't meant to be at that time.

I stayed on with Private Jet Expeditions, flying for a month or so. The daily boredom did not fade away. Lots of good people worked for the company, but this older pilot had gotten so used to the non-automated aircraft with their "steam gauges" that he just could not reach a comfort zone. The flying was really no different from the previous vacation-charter flying I did prior to taking on the bush flying.

I finally asked for a leave of absence. I collapsed into practically nothingness, yet I continued to keep an eye peeled for another aviation experience at a later date. In the belief that a little R & R might take care of the problem, the lull severely worsened the situation. I started patronizing the local bars much too frequently, drinking and smoking too much, and setting aside my normal exercise routine. I really did not need to work at that time because I still drew checks earned during the Angola operation.

Av Atlantic

In early 1995, I received a call from a company called AV Atlantic, which operated 727s out of Savanna, Georgia. Somebody had given them my name along with a good recommendation as an experienced 727 captain. The aircraft were actually B-727-200s, the stretched version. They needed someone qualified for international flying and check-captain duties, both of which sounded right up my alley. Of greater importance, the position allowed me to slip immediately into the captain's seat again to further the kind of flying that I so enjoyed.

I jumped headlong into the offer and headed to Savanna, Georgia, for *another* ground school. Every time you change airplanes, you have to do the required recurrent training, and this one would hardly cause a whisper of a breeze primarily because I had already been teaching Boeing 727 systems for several years. I was still fifty-eight years of age at the time and didn't really have too much longer to fly as a pilot in a FAR 121 operation as the maximum age limit for commercial pilots at that time was sixty years (it has since been increased to sixty-five). I pretty well had it in my head that this new employment would wind up as my curtain call—my last flying adventure.

A family-owned company, two daughters led the operation, taking control, so I heard when their father either became unable to handle the operations or retired. AV Atlantic functioned to fly passengers on island-hopping vacations, including flights to Mexico and other non-island vacation destinations, quite similar, in fact, to other airlines I had flown for in the past.

I found myself excitedly looking forward to a an anticipated contract between AV Atlantic and a British company called Airtours International, whose fleet consisted of MD-80 aircraft. One of its planes had landed gear up, and the company needed AV Atlantic's assistance to fly its passengers during the airplane's repair. Airtours, much like AV Atlantic, operated as a vacation-charter company that made trips to Tenerife-South and Fuerteventura in the Canary Islands, to Zakynthos and Iraklion in Greece as well as European routes to Reus and Minorca in Spain and Faro in Portugal.

Many of you may well recall Tenerife as the unfortunate host for the deadliest crash in aviation history when two 747s collided on the runway. This tragic accident resulted from a combination of pea-soup fog that engulfed the airport facility, more than a bit of miscommunication between the crews and ATC, and a captain, in my view, hell-bent on getting "out-of-town."

The KLM 747 initiated its takeoff roll with another aircraft, a passenger-filled Pan Am 747, still on the runway. Exactly 583 people lost their lives on March 27, 1977. Fortunately, sixty-one people aboard Pan Am's 747 managed somehow to live to tell their story. No one aboard KLM's aircraft survived. While flying airplanes is inherently safe, aviation often remains vulnerable to the smallest of errors!

Getting back to my next—and most likely last—aviation employer, AV Atlantic, the company finalized the contract with Airtours International and began to assemble flight crews. A gentleman named Eddie Grue, one of the family members who owned the airline, would become my flight engineer, along with three other complete flight crews and an entire gaggle of flight attendants.

On our initial flight, we were to go to Goose Bay, then on to Keflavik, Iceland, and finally to London's Stansted Airport. Keflavik hosted a Naval Air Station that also housed USAF, USMC, and US Army operations, functioning as a relay station for military and commercial flights to Europe. The weather was always unpredictable there, so much so that it was not unusual to receive an airborne clear-weather report only to run into zero visibility on landing.

We gathered all the crews and supplies and prepared for departure from Savanna, Georgia. Since my crew would be first at bat, we put the initial flight plan together, somewhat of a hassle because this flight amounted to the company's initial entrance into this kind of flying operation. From my perspective, it was just old stuff because I had already completed such missions with the USAF and civilian companies numerous times. I figured we had on board enough crews, maintenance people, and company representatives to operate for at least a month.

Our first leg brought us without incident to Goose Bay, Labrador, for our first fuel stop. Everything operated unbelievably well. Because I had landed there many times in the past, I knew the surrounding terrain: a vast wilderness dotted by a few lakes not visible during wintertime because of the vast snow cover. We set the bird down at Goose Bay Air Force Base, established in 1952 to house the 95th Strategic Wing of the Strategic Air Command (SAC). Far from a desirable duty station, military folks favored this expression when assigned there: "Up Goose Creek without a paddle."

Considering the remoteness of our first and second destination, I again bring to mind the aviator's adage, "The only time you have too much fuel is when you are on fire." In areas like Labrador and Iceland, you never knew what to expect from the weather at any given time. Hence, the pilot made sure to add a little extra fuel for the "wife and kids." Even though Keflavik, our next scheduled destination, showed a favorable weather forecast, I did not count on it; therefore, I topped this baby off with the maximum amount of jet fuel, although making us a little heavy for takeoff.

We reassembled and prepared for a day-time flight to Keflavik. Our flight attendants provided excellent service, perhaps even pulling out and distributing some of the "best stuff" on board. We did not want for food.

To pass the time away, a number of the passengers played poker. Our flight schedule and fuel burn proceeded without a single glitch.

Once we began to close in on Iceland, we turned over to Keflavik approach, predictably advising to look forward to worsened weather and a very low ceiling. At the same time, a Navy P-3 attempted unsuccessfully to land and had to execute a missed approach. Tuning in on the same radio frequency, we overheard the turn-over to departure after the Navy plane missed its first approach.

I knew we had enough fuel for a couple of approaches; however, if we couldn't make the landing, we also did not want to have to divert to Reykjavik. Yes, without doubt we could *land* at Reykjavik, but we would most certainly encounter problems in *taking off* again with such a heavy load, making it pretty much imperative to land at Keflavik. Again, the P-3 failed on its next approach. Clearly, we needed to put down there, and Captain Mullins would have to carve out the best approach he had ever made before.

I finally requested a go, cautioning my crew to stay cool yet tight on the approach and to advise me of *anything* going wrong. Experience taught me to maintain three sets of eyes and ears in such situations. We were vectored for the ILS approach, ears glued to the headsets, eyes focused on the instruments. As the copilot communicated with control during approach, I flew the machine, and so far all looked okay. Even the radio communications reached our ears with a quality unknown to me during my African-bush days. Control also provided us with very satisfactory wide turns to final, an important advantage when flying in to these areas.

Very professional people, these base controllers had to cope with such conditions nearly every day. As we drew closer, control gave us a right turn to an intercept heading for the ILS. The copilot heard one heading-change call but I heard another; subsequently, I requested the copilot to ask for a repeat. Because I had heard correctly, I had to caution him, since the exact call could mean the difference between success and failure under such conditions.

I maneuvered us to the ILS, with the glide slope just slightly above the bar, exactly where I wanted it. I planned to fly the approach with the needles crossed exactly as they were, holding a little extra air speed for mom and the kids. I knew we would not encounter any African landing-strip embankments around the end of the runway, feeling confidant, in fact, to drop a little below minimums if necessary. The needles held perfectly on center when we passed through 100 feet above minimums, and we prepared to negotiate new minimums at fifty feet.

All of us in the cockpit attempted to visualize the runway. Nothing yet. Hyperventilation intensified. With the needles still crossed, I dropped down, finding ourselves at the underside of the cloud layer. In a split second, the runway *finally* came into view.

"In sight!" exclaimed the flight engineer. Lady luck again accompanied me on this day, particularly when I observed that we headed straight down the centerline! I made an unusually smooth landing, quite common when concentrating to get this thing down.

Since we'd have to spend some time during refuel, I invited everyone to leave the plane to stretch out their legs. The next leg would involve the shortest leg, and the other two crews agreed to split the time.

"Colder than a witch's tit on an iceberg," the Klondike's environment displayed nothing but snow on top of more snow. Of course, no one wore appropriate clothing for this kind of weather. I laughed a bit when I saw shivering shapes quickly running to the terminal.

The terminal offered shops to purchase local artifacts, magazines, newspapers, among a host of things for sale. Lots of folks, I observed, bought locally produced relics if only to claim that they had landed there for a visit.

Finding myself in the terminal as well, I called to mind the vast number of approaches I had made over the past several years. Many took place under virtually the same conditions as this one at Keflavik; to be sure, many greatly resembled experiences in piloting those KC-97s back and forth to Germany, attempting to land safely during low ceilings and next-to-nothing visibility.

I also remembered the times we landed here at Keflavik and at Goose Bay over the course of my aviation career. Once we had silenced the engines after parking the aircraft, we grimaced at the walls of extraordinarily high snow banks created alongside the runway by heavy-duty snow plows, beautiful white embankments that *also* decreased depth perception on landing.

On a positive note, we spent some pretty good layovers there at Goose Bay club. Usually packed with male and female civilian school teachers there on contract, the club served as an interesting party house, which *The Blues Brothers* John Belushi would have enjoyed had he himself survived. Back then, most of us guys had not yet hit our 30s; partying, therefore, was right up our alley.

The AV Atlantic people and I then concluded the transatlantic flight to London. A company bus picked us up and delivered us to our hotel nestled away in a small, suburban community located a good chunk of miles distant from the airport. We checked in and commenced a local tour, locating, of course, a number of pleasant, little pubs within walking distance of our sleeping quarters. Unsurprisingly, we checked a few of them out that afternoon, concluding that these British blokes numbered among the heaviest beer drinkers on the planet, actually exceeding my own limitations! Yes, we had found yet another fun place.

After an evening of "By Jove! You Yanks like to have fun!" we awoke the next morning, showered, put on fresh clothing, ate breakfast, and headed to a company briefing to determine routes and other need-to-know information. Among other things, we learned we would fly to several destinations, all vacation-resort areas located along coastal waters.

Fuel consumption concerned both crewmembers and company officials because the MD-80s would have to make fuel stops on most of the trips. The 727s that AV Atlantic flew, I explained, because of their greater range, would not need to refuel prior to reaching a number of destinations. We agreed, of course, to initiate things their way at first since they held onto the purse strings. If we did not have to land to refuel, we argued, we would certainly increase the number of trips as well as save them money.

"*Geld regiert die Welt*," asserts one character out of German playwright Bertolt Brecht's *The Three Penny Opera*, namely that "Money rules the world."

While the Airtours reps most likely had little understanding of the nuances posed by literary works, the proposal sounded good to them. It went without saying that we would require a full load of fuel for each takeoff. If our concepts proved sound and safe, they yielded to the things we could do in order to operate more economically and efficiently. We really could not make any determinations though until we began to carry out our flying assignments.

As noted earlier, our destinations included Fuerteventura and Tenerife-South in the Canary Islands, Faro in Portugal, Reus and Minorca in Spain, and Zakynthos and Iraklion in Greece, all coastline vacation resorts.

Our first trip out of London would head to Tenerife in the Canary Islands. Eddie Grue, who held ownership shares in the company, accompanied us as flight engineer. Tina, the senior flight attendant, helped service passengers along with cabin colleagues Lisa and Tyra Grimes. My copilot's name has now slipped into the forever-gone closet in my brain.

We gathered our belongings, and the hotel's bus delivered us to Stansted Airport, formerly a once proud Royal Air Force base used by the USAF Eighth Air Force to carry out B-17 and B-26 bombing missions over Germany during World War II. The base also boasted a prisoner-of-war facility to house Germans captured at the time.

One of three major airports in London (plus Heathrow and Gatwick), Stansted was originally set up for cargo, non-scheduled charter operators, and corporate aviation out of a private terminal. In 1986 the British government allocated a large grant to develop the airport, and it has grown since then to become the third busiest airport in the UK.

European operational procedures differed in one important way from those in the USA. Instead of starting the engines and making the taxi out to the runway to line up for takeoff, European standards made us wait for a "block time" even before firing up the engines. I much preferred this technique over sitting and waiting out there on the taxiway; besides, the procedure reduced ground time and saved valuable fuel, thus cutting down on operational costs and saving just enough to avoid an en-route fuel stop. I also appreciated the low-altitude speed restrictions.

The faster you flew on the approach to the airports, the better they liked it. It was not unusual for controllers to request airspeed of 300 knots as long as possible, which I enjoyed very much. I also really liked the way they handled the traffic, resulting in much more efficiency in comparison to America's FAA-regulated ATC system.

I did have one big problem with French female controllers whose shrill voices could slice my ear drums in half. Then, too, I had difficulty adjusting to their French accent, frequently requesting a repeat because I did not want to draw conclusions based on assumptions. My copilot *also* had problems understanding them. The flight engineer, on the other hand, could comprehend them most of the time, so I would use him as a translator. Once again, that third crewmember, the flight engineer, would come galloping gallantly to the rescue!

Pulling away now from this digression, I point out that we arrived in Tenerife without incident. The main runway was plenty long enough to accommodate the aircraft, its cargo and crew, and a full load of fuel. Because we intended to demonstrate to the company on this non-stop flight in the Boeing 727 that we could do the job well—or better—we agreed, my flight crewmembers and I, to make an attempt to get back to Stansted without a fuel stop.

If we succeeded, then our effort could *only* put us in a very good light. I nudged the flaps just slightly lower than the normal takeoff position just to be on the safe side, an action which worked out just fine as we got airborne with no problems. We didn't have any complications making it all the way to Stansted without a fuel stop, saving the company a bunch of money and allowing us to put a little feather in our company hats.

The next trip would go to Faro, Portugal, quite a bit shorter, and a place where the ground-handler guy began to take a considerable liking to my flight attendant, Tina. On every trip there, he would get into her space, respectfully, of course, as much as possible. One day he *actually* asked me if he could have her. Attempting to stay outwardly serious yet laughing my butt off inwardly, I let the guy know that I'd offer Tina in place of one of the cute, little *chicas* ("chicks" in English) who worked in the office there.

In time, this trade-off deal turned into a grand joke among Tina, me, and the rest of the crewmembers. For Tina's side, she simply laughed it off, the good sport that she was. As for the ground handler, I did believe he earnestly wanted to make a trade, understandably so, because Tina really stood out as a good-looking, short but pretty well stacked, blonde-haired lady. Who could blame the guy for his desires?

We were on a trip to Iraklion, Greece, one night about "dark thirty" when Eddie kidded around with the flight attendants. He believed he had convinced them that we were flying near the Bosnian no-fly zone, warning them to watch out for flaming telephone poles (SAMs) coming toward the plane. As we flew southbound along the boot of Italy, we were re-cleared to a point that was not on our flight plan, and we had difficulties locating it.

About the same time, Tina opened the door to the cockpit to hear Eddie cry out, "Where the F*** are we!" Now understandably aroused (and certainly not from the libido's point of view), she darted off and advised the other flight attendants to watch out the windows for the SAMs! Not amused, the flight attendants, most likely stemming from similar episodes on other flights over their careers, wrote off Eddie's ploy as a way to create a bit of flight-crew playfulness, which ended the next day when the company's chief pilot wanted to know which crew member didn't know where the F*** he was.

On a night-time flight to Zakynthos, one of Greece's splendid islands located in the Ionian Sea, the handlers claimed that our arrival had blown off the roof of a recently constructed house near the end of the runway. In response, I stated that the house must have been one of those small, concrete-block shacks with a metal roof, held down with additional concrete blocks—a rudimentary, architectural technique often used to reduce building costs. Reasonably certain of the lack of zoning here, Eddie joined the conversation, pointing out that he had seen the building, arguing point blank that the structure had been built far too close to the runway. Nothing more came out of the incident, much like the bush-whacking event a number of years earlier in Angola.

We flew this operation for a while until Airtours got the MD-80 repaired and back on line. We made some real good scores during our European stint and received high ratings from the company. We then flew the 727 back to Savanna for another assignment with AV Atlantic, an operation out of the windy, cold, icy city of Chicago.

The flights consisted of the same old vacation-tour-group flights to Mexico, to the Caribbean, to Las Vegas, and to Long Beach, California.

The Long Beach flights were carried out for another outfit that leased the planes but mostly used its own flying crews. Some of the guys crossed over from Private Jet Expeditions when that company flopped.

In this aviation business, irony sometimes begets irony. One of the cross-over guys had been *my* check captain when I worked for Private Jet Expeditions, and now I was checking *him* out to fly for our operation! To add irony on top of irony, my newest company also hired a young, female pilot who had helped fund PJE's operations. We figured she represented the "private" part of Private Jet Expeditions.

We used the Northwest Airlines (NATCO) training facility in Minneapolis for check-out training, a place always as cold as "a well digger's ass in the Klondike." Despite the coldness and the intended simile, the operation ran quite smoothly. We functioned with two crews, and we kept each crew together for all of the flights, a strategy that also worked very well. Aviation research has conclusively revealed that a flight crew that has worked together for a long time is far more effective than a brand-new crew flying together for the first time.

Long Beach's airport was very sensitive regarding noise-abatement procedures, making flights out of there difficult to fly without setting off the facility's very sensitive alarm at least once or twice. The company would always get a notification from the FAA when my crew and I had "rung the bell" a few times. An accumulation of too many violations would result in a fine of several thousand dollars. When the second crew began to fly, the warnings appeared to increase somewhat; as a consequence, company officials, we heard, had to have a "word" (an ass-chewing) with the crew members.

At the time, I spent about as much time in the simulator performing flight training as I did during real-time flying. We would either use simulators at American in Dallas, Texas, or Northwest in Minneapolis, Minnesota, both excellent training facilities.

On January 17, 1996, Grey Ghost's pilot made his final round-trip flight from Chicago to Long Beach, California, under the FAR Part 121 rules at the young age of sixty. After the return flight, I checked into the motel to participate in a small party organized for me by the rest of my crew. I think we partied until the wee hours of the morning. When I woke up the next morning, my throbbing head notified me that I had enjoyed a really good party. I then headed to the airport to claim a jump-seat ride with KIA Airlines from Chicago to Atlanta. As radio personality Paul Harvey might have said, "And *soooo*, my friends, that's the *ennnnnd* of the story."

While it's true that my piloting days had concluded, I was fortunate enough to have amassed a great deal of flight-training and simulator experience, allowing me to accept employment with a few companies in their training departments. I went on to work for Av Atlantic, Nations Air, and Aero Services in Miami for a few additional years. I was also qualified at Northwest (NATCO), but I didn't particularly like to go there due to the cold weather.

Despite the opportunities to help train crew members, I still found myself sitting restlessly at home, hanging out at local bars, drinking, and smoking too heavily even during employment gaps. My new-found instructor's position did not produce long-standing, full-time employment, and those checks from my Angola days had ceased to arrive years earlier.

Finally, when things really began to look desperate for me, AV Atlantic, my previous employer when I had to call it quits as a pilot, telephoned me in 1996 to ask if I would like to continue simulator training. Nothing in FAR regulations suggested that I could not perform such work. In fact, I would only need a 3rd class medical certificate to make a go of it. They had several guys who were due for recurrent training at the time, and they wanted my services to train them on the simulators at Aero Services in Miami. I considered the offer a perfectly cut piece of cake because I had already trained on these same simulators back in the late 70s and early 80s, right there on 36th street, the hub of activity for Miami International Airport for more than fifty years.

The company put me and the gang up at the Ho Jo's, located very close to the training facility. We pretty much had a choice of day or night simulator usage. I would often stay there for a couple of weeks, return home to the family for a few days, then head back to Miami for another couple of weeks from 1996 until 1998, continually rotating in this manner from month to month. The crews were staggered for their training, and it was very unusual to have more than two weeks off at a time. Each training period consisted of about two hours of classroom instruction and four hours on the simulator.

We carried out the training in Miami for a while until something happened, and we were relocated to the American training facility at Dallas, Texas. Normally, when this took place, the situation almost always revolved around money—quite frequently simulator cost, travel cost, or hotel expense. If the truth be told, it was common practice for the small, fly-by-night airlines to run up a big bill at a hotel, to "burn the bill," and to shift their crews to other locations.

The move to Dallas did not really make a difference to us because we considered Dallas a very good place for training. Besides, we stayed at a motel quite close to the baseball stadium used by the Texas Rangers. The area also looked decent and supported lots of fine little bars and restaurants within walking distance. In addition, the motel sported a big swimming pool right in the center of the facility where we could lounge, study flight manuals, empty a few bottles of beer, and ogle the bathing beauties attempting to tan themselves.

I was very well known at this motel, as it was the same one we used when I was with Independent Air doing the 707 training. I would always get the room I liked at the rear of the pool, the perfect location to provide a panoramic view as well as an ongoing look at the bikini-clad "eye candy" lying around the pool. In addition, the motel's bar and lounge offered opportunities to meet lots of available southern sugar babies. As a matter of fact, our days there took place during the era of the line-dance fad that had everyone on their toes on Saturday nights twisting and turning to the tunes of a good old country music band made up of pickers and singers.

Honestly, after a weekend there, it was hard to get the boys motivated on Monday. Some of them would even get lost at some sweet-young-thing's house. Usually though, someone knew where to find these temporarily lost souls, most likely, I reasoned, because they had already been there themselves.

The simulator periods typically began at midnight and lasted until six the next morning because American used the facility for its own purposes or the company had to perform maintenance on the machines during the day. Such a schedule *did* encourage some of us to slip into a mode of drinking and smoking too much, not to mention all the other bad habits that could lure people who had distanced themselves from their "healthier" habits at home.

When the night's training came to an end, we'd head over to the "greasy spoon" across the street from the motel for an old-fashioned, high-calorie, high-carbohydrate, high-fat breakfast. This hedonistic session paved the way for at least an hour to put away a glass or two of alcoholic beverages in order to help us sleep, we presumed, before hitting the sack during daylight hours. And such a schedule, if I permit myself to use the word, continued in the same way for instructional session after instructional session. Because I no longer worried about passing a six-month medical exam for piloting, I went on engorging my body with all the wrong stuff.

From time to time, however, I did get a chance to fly the airplane for an FAA-required captain's up-grade. We would first position ourselves wherever the airplane sat at the time. On one occasion, I went to Miami for a check ride. To paraphrase an old expression, what went around could come around again: the FAA examiner turned out to be a fellow named Jim Reddy, with whom I had flown at both Air Atlanta and Gulf Air.

Elated to run into each other again, we soon lost the joy of the reunion when we learned that the maintenance people were still doing maintenance on the aircraft that would be used for the check ride, and no one bothered to notify us. After a few "expletives deleted," Jim, a calm and cool guy, said, "Not to worry about it—we'll wait until they finish the maintenance."

With those words behind us, we headed over to Wag's restaurant on 36th street for coffee and chat about the old times, requesting the guys to fetch us at completion. Jim, like my own experience, spent a good deal of time in the non-sked business and, like me, took on the demeanor of the world-wide traveler insisting he had "been there and done that."

The maintenance guys finally arrived to pick us up for the check ride. We only had one aviator to check at the time, so the process wouldn't take very long. We boarded, took off, and cruised over to the Dade Collier Training Center (TNT), an airport located about forty miles west of MIA. It was a night-time flight, and there was no one else around TNT at that time of night, not even an air traffic controller.

We simply used the required frequency for the transmissions needed for any other traffic that might show up. The fellow involved in the check ride completed everything required for a successful ride, and I proudly rejoiced with the idea that "I taught him well."

After we completed the check, I asked Jim, as a courtesy, if he would like to fly the airplane back to Miami. Knowing that these FAA "fellahs" seldom have the opportunity to pilot an air machine, I figured Jim would happily take me up on the offer. After we landed in Miami, we thanked him, he left, and I have yet to see him again. A classic "salt-of-the-earth" non-skedder, Jim had flown with Continental before the strike. He also spent time as a management pilot with Air Atlanta, always reaching out to help people.

I continued the same line of business for a couple more years until the companies finally went the way of most of these small, fly-by-night airlines into their "TU" or "tits-up" phase of termination, usually through a chapter 11 proceeding, which left employees, in particular, without already earned pay and very little chance to recoup.

In 1998, I performed my last instructional job with Nations Air, another start-up company located in Atlanta and owned by Mark McDonald, with whom I had flown at Independent Air. Gil Ramsden, the director of operations, had also flown with me at other airlines.

CHAPTER FOURTEEN

CONCLUSION

I feel very fortunate to have been able to come out of a mountainous, coal-mining area with only a high school education and to have been able to accomplish the things I did. I was destined to become a pilot and one day to fulfill my dream to command the B-707 by whatever means necessary. Since I had no college under my belt, most of the things I needed to learn to accomplish put me back to the basics, starting from scratch, you might say.

We did not have access to computers in those days; instead, we relied on the slide rule for mathematical calculations, an important tool in aviation studies. What did I have going for me back then? I possessed a strong motivation to accomplish my goals.

The United States Air Force introduced me to the beginning of my aviation career as a flight engineer. What I learned from the Air Force experience enabled me to push forward toward successful entry into the world of actual piloting. The Air Force experience also resulted in a favorable pension, which I began to draw at the age of sixty, my reward for all those years working for "the big uncle." Finally, the Air Force experience qualified me to make use of the GI Bill to expedite education in my civilian flight training.

I am thankful to have had the opportunity given me to be able to travel around the world as I did, and getting paid for what I loved to do. I met many fine people, my "brothers and sisters," along the way, and many represented immense, walking treasures.

I have had the opportunity to meet several celebrities on my path towards my dream of sitting in the captain's seat of the big, sleek Boeing 707: Robert Mitchum, Charles Bronson, Chuck Yeager, Chuck Norris, Bruce Springsteen, Tim Conway, Maria Osmond, Ray Stevens, Hank Williams Jr., and many others.

Nowadays, I spend time playing in my little bicycle shop set up in the garage. I love to tinker with the old three-speed antique bikes. After a heart attack in 2008, I came to realize that the time had come to give up the bad habits of drinking and smoking, replacing them with a healthier lifestyle. I have found the importance of eating right and exercising. Pat, my wife, steadfastly remains my greatest supporter and motivator.

My travels now consist of walking two to three miles a day or taking my bike out on the riding trails. Last summer my wife and I pedaled the total distance of the Silver Comet Trail, which runs from Smyrna, Georgia, to the Alabama line, covering about sixty-one miles. We actually doubled the distance on each occasion when we cycled from one point to another and back. The longest ride we made in one day covered about forty-one miles. It took us about four Sundays to cover the complete distance to the Alabama line. When I flew the jets, I could travel the same distance in about five minutes.

I sincerely hope you enjoyed reading my autobiographical narrative. If I live long enough, perhaps I'll boot up the computer to fashion another account at a later date. God bless you all.

GLOSSARY

A/C–aircraft commander; the military term for captain of the airplane or pilot in command

ADF–automatic direction finder; using a beacon (or bearing or radio transmission), a marine or aircraft radio-navigation instrument that automatically and continuously displays the relative bearing from the ship or aircraft to a suitable radio station

AFB–Air Force base

ATC–air traffic control

Beta Range–the area between high and low on a turbo prop, allowing the pilot to control the pitch of the blades for power changes

Buckets–located on the perimeter of the jet-engine turbine wheel, buckets are small, floating airfoil tabs that create a forward motion when the engine is turning

Check Point Charley Navigation–navigation by coordinates and Oceanic Control

Come alongs–similar to a "block and tackle," a rope or cable device that uses pulleys with ropes or cables to move very heavy items

Dark thirty–late in the evening or anytime between midnight and daylight

DO–director of operations; the person who oversees the entirety of an aviation operation

FL–flight level; a prefix to a three-digit number that represents thousands of feet above sea level; example: FL 330 represents 33,000 feet above sea level

George–a pilot's nickname for the aircraft's autopilot

Hercules–the nickname for the C-130 aircraft, a four-engine turboprop cargo carrier

Ibos–Biafran natives

ILS–instrument landing system; the primary mode of navigation for landing during low visibility and ceilings, allowing the pilots to fly their aircraft along an electronic path that takes them to the centerline of the runway to a point located 1,000 feet from the approach end of the runway

IOE–initial operating experience; the training required for an airline pilot to be fully qualified

KLM–a Dutch airline that operates worldwide

Oceanic Control–an antiquated method of air traffic control that requires the en-route pilots to report their position to a ground-based facility (no radar) in order for Oceanic Control to plot the locations for traffic separation; only used when there is no radar available

ORI–operational readiness inspection; when an overseeing command agency initiates a no-notice inspection of a given military organization to determine its fitness

OJT–on-the-job training

On-schedule–a reference to the aircraft manufacturer's recommended speeds at which to extend or to retract items such as landing gear and flaps

Pone–a chunk of cornbread baked in a metal skillet

Southern Air Transport–an airline that is primarily funded and/or operated by the CIA

SAC–Strategic Air Command; the branch of the Air force that operates large B-52 aircraft and is primarily responsible for the airplanes that drop nuclear weapons

Sanford and Son–a TV show that featured a father and son who ran a junkyard; the book compares an aviation entrepreneur and his son to the main characters in *Sanford and Son*

TI–training instructor; the person in a military-training environment responsible for training new recruits; sometimes referred to as the DI, or drill instructor

T-6–a World War II, single-engine, propeller-driven aircraft still flown extensively throughout the world

VOR–shortened form for VHF Omni-directional range; a type of short-range, radio navigation system for aircraft to determine their position and to stay on course by receiving radio signals transmitted by a network of fixed-group radio beacons to the aircraft's receiver unit

V1–the speed on takeoff roll representing a go or a no-go point; if an engine failure occurs below that speed, the pilot must abort the takeoff; if an engine failure occurs above that speed, the pilot must continue the takeoff

Vr–the speed at which the pilot initiates control inputs for liftoff

V2–the speed used for climb if an engine fails after takeoff

WAG–wild-ass guess; pilot slang for making an educated guess that can't be quantified